Keeping
and Breeding
Snakes

Keeping and Breeding Snakes

Chris Mattison

BLANDFORD

First published in the UK 1996 by Cassell Plc,
Wellington House, 125 Strand, London, WC2R OBB.

Previously published in the UK in hardback 1988 by
Blandford Press.

Reprinted 1989, 1992, 1994

Distribution in the United States
by Sterling Publishing Co., Inc.
387 Park Avenue South, New York,
NY 10016-8810

Distribution in Australia
by Capricorn Link (Australia) Pty Ltd
2/13 Carrington Road, Castle Hill NSW 2154

A British Library Cataloguing in Publication Data

Mattison, Christopher
Keeping and breeding snakes.
1. Pets: Snakes, Breeding & care
1. Title
639.3'96

ISBN 0-7137-2579-6

Typeset at the Alden Press. Oxford, London and Northampton
Printed and bound in Hong Kong by South China Printing Co Ltd

Contents

Acknowledgements

In order to compile the information which is presented in this book I have drawn on the experiences, written and verbal, of many persons who are more expert in the field of snake-keeping than myself. To these people, many of whom are referred to in the references throughout the text, I offer my gratitude. In addition I extend my thanks to all of those who have responded to my requests for information and breeding data – their names will be found next to the appropriate headings. In this connection, Robert Applegate deserves special mention for allowing me free access to his extensive breeding records from which I was able to obtain valuable information, especially on several of the rarely-seen tri-coloured kingsnakes and milk snakes.

Others have loaned literature, pointed out sources of information and given general encouragement. It is not possible to list them all, but they know who they are, and I can only hope they will realise that their contributions to this project have been highly valued.

Of the photographs, many were taken at the homes of private individuals who generously allowed me to handle, pose and generally mess about with their animals, many of them valuable, all of them treasured. Others were photographed at zoos, with the assistance of their keepers. Details are listed below:

Bob Applegate: colour plates 12, 13, 15, 16, 17; black and white plates 1, 2, Jon Coote: black and white plate 16, Cotswold Wildlife Park (Nigel Platt): colour plate 25; black and white plates 7, 10, 28, Cotswold Wildlife Park (Don Reid): colour plate 39, Ray Hine: colour plates 1, 4, 6, 24; black and white plate 11, Mike Nolan: colour plates 5, 7, 14, 22, 26, 32, 33, 34, 35; black and white plates 6, 8, 12, 13, 21, Nick Nyoka: colour plate 8, Charles Samson/Michelle Course: colour plate 2; black and white plate 9, San Diego Zoo (Charles Radcliffe): colour plates 3, 30; black and white plate 29, Gary Sipperley: black and white plate 14.

The remaining snakes were either in my care at the time, or wild. Wild snakes were found and photographed with the aid of Robert Applegate, Pete Carmichael and Bill Montgomery.

Finally, I am delighted to be able to acknowledge the help of my daughter, Victoria, in preparing many of the line drawings.

Introduction

In 1967 one of Britain's leading herpetologists, Professor Angus Bellairs, wrote (correctly) 'It is hardly surprising that the behaviour of reptiles in captivity is often a travesty of that in nature. They are likely to become sluggish and refuse to feed, eventually dying of starvation. They seldom breed, so that stock can only be replenished by purchase or collection of fresh specimens.' Twenty years on, that statement could hardly be further from the truth: tens of thousands of reptiles are being bred each year by zoological gardens, scientific institutions and, especially, by amateur herpetologists.

Although lizards and turtles have also figured in this revolution, the most spectacular progress to date has been in the breeding of snakes, and it is now apparent that practically any species can be successfully maintained and bred in captivity, provided only that there is sufficient will to do so.

The reasons for this change are threefold. Firstly, an awareness of the plight of wild creatures in general has led to the realisation that 're-plenishment by purchase or collection of fresh specimens' can no longer be justified *ad infinitum*. Secondly, the conditions under which our animals are kept have improved, due partly to the availability of sophis-ticated equipment (often borrowed from other hobbies) for heating and illuminating them. Finally, and most significantly, the gradual but steadily growing interest in the keeping of reptiles has extended to individuals who are well adapted intellectually to overcome former problems in husbandry by the application of a sound scientific under-standing of the biology of these strange but interesting animals.

With these three components we now have: a good reason to breed reptiles; the equipment with which to do it; and the people to show us how to go about it. Indeed, a recent and welcome development is the establishment of commercial and semi-commercial snake-breeding operations whose sum effect has been to meet the demand for certain popular species, improve the standard of animals being offered for sale and bring the prices even of formerly 'rare' species down to a level where they are more easily affordable.

Information on the successful keeping and breeding of snakes is therefore accumulating rapidly, but until now this has appeared only in numerous society publications and magazines. Some of these are well known but others are obscure and no longer readily available. The purpose of this book is to bring together data and information from as wide a range of sources as possible, to summarise it, and to present it in a form which will make it more readily accessible.

As far as is possible, I have included every aspect of snake husbandry which is necessary to keep most of the species that the hobbyist is likely to encounter. Many of the fundamental principles of snake-keeping are common to all or most species and these are explained in Chapters 1–6. It is important that these are read in conjunction with the species accounts (Chapters 7–12) since the latter are abbreviated in order to avoid repetition. The accounts themselves are a summary of the information which is available on each particular species. This information has been obtained from three sources: personal experience; published papers and articles; and notes supplied by a large number of experienced snake-keepers. Wherever possible, a 'key' reference has been given for each species or group of species in order that the reader can research his or her animals more thoroughly.

It is important to realise, however, that there are two variables involved in snake-keeping. Firstly, snakes are living organisms and, as such, may differ from one another, even within species. Thus the information supplied may not apply to every individual – this is especially so in the case of species which have not been widely kept – and so some experimentation may be necessary. Secondly, snake-keepers are also living organisms and are also subject to variation. Some people seem to have a natural affinity with captive snakes and succeed where others fail, and methods which work for one person do not always work for another. Therefore, nothing which is stated in this book should be regarded as categorical – many species which were formerly regarded as 'impossible' are now being bred regularly and, to some extent, some of the species which are often recommended for beginners have turned out to be among the most difficult to keep in the long term.

Finally, advances in the science of animal husbandry are being made almost every day. This means that this book will not become 'the last word' in snake-keeping, but only an account of the state of snake-keeping at one point in time; in fact it will begin to date even before it is published.

One of the reasons that snakes are now kept more successfully than ever before is that information-sharing has become an important part of our hobby. In order to gain access to this information it is usually necessary to join one or more of the societies which are listed in Appendix II. Furthermore, it is equally important that other hobbyists are made aware of your successes (and failures). In over twenty years of keeping a wide variety of species I have been fortunate in receiving advice, ideas and suggestions from very many people. I hope that by passing on some of these ideas through this book I shall be doing a service not only to people who keep snakes, but also to the animals which have given me so much enjoyment.

CHAPTER 1

First Principles

There are two ways of learning how to do something. It can be learned by rote; in other words, instructions compiled by someone else can be followed to the letter; or it can be learned by becoming familiar with the underlying principles. Learning to drive a car is a good example of the first method – very few drivers know, or wish to know, how the various components work, or how they combine to make the car go. Keeping snakes can also be learned like this, by following each procedure step-by-step, but by far the best results are obtained by understanding how snakes live – what makes them tick. This enables the keeper to cope with unexpected complications, improve on techniques which others have developed, or develop entirely new techniques. It also turns the animals into objects of interest rather than merely unusual pets.

This chapter, then, is directed towards those people who have little or no biological background and little or no experience in keeping snakes. To knowledgeable keepers, many of the points made will be obvious and much of the advice will have become instinctive.

Because snakes are wild animals, rather than domesticated pets, it is important to have a basic grasp of their biological requirements before any attempt can be made to provide suitable living conditions for them. In addition, if the maximum enjoyment is to be had from keeping them, it is equally important to look a little more closely into their natural history than would be the case with 'ordinary' pets which are far removed from their wild ancestors.

The snakes form one suborder of the animals known as reptiles, which also includes the turtles, the tuatara, crocodiles and lizards. As far as we can tell, the first snakes evolved from their lizard-like ancestors about 120 million years ago. Their most obvious feature – the lack of limbs – is due to the exclusively burrowing habits of these primitive snakes; and other parts of their anatomy, the eyes, eyelids and ear-openings, also became superfluous and therefore degenerated for the same reason. The body became elongated and the number of ribs increased accordingly, while the internal organs were reshaped and repositioned to fit into the new shape. Several families of snakes still contain burrowing, or fossorial, species, but the more advanced families re-emerged from beneath the ground and diversified to fill other evolutionary niches – the earth's surface, the trees, the rivers and lakes and the oceans. Since organs which are lost through the evolutionary process are never regained in the same form, this 'new generation' of snakes had to manage without limbs, efficient eyes or ears, although other organs were developed to compensate. These are unique to snakes and consist of Jacobson's organ, a paired cavity in the roof of the mouth which is connected to the olfactory system and identifies airborne scent particles collected by the snake's flickering tongue, and the facial pits found among the boas and pythons and the pit vipers, which are sensitive to the heat radiated by warm-blooded animals in the vicinity.

Furthermore, the loss of limbs has never appeared to be of any great disadvantage to snakes as they have developed a number of alternative means of locomotion to suit their size and habitat. These include the typical serpentine movement used when moving over rough ground or when swimming; 'straight-line' (rectilinear) locomotion used by heavy-bodied snakes; and sidewinding, a method used by desert species to move across a loose, shifting substrate. Most species can climb, and some of them are very adept at this. All snakes (except possibly the primitive worm and thread snakes) also appear to be able to swim, although some are more at home in the water than others; these may be recognisable by upward-pointing eyes and nostrils and, in a few cases, a flattened tail. Burrowing species usually have smooth, shiny scales and may also have a wedge-shaped snout and a short, blunt tail.

A more immediate variation between the species, and one which will probably be more significant to the prospective keeper, is that of colour and markings. The various patterns serve a purpose and are not randomly assigned to each species for the benefit of snake-keepers. Most snakes are camouflaged in order to blend in with their natural surroundings, although this may not be immediately obvious when the substrate is artificial. Brown snakes are usually ground-dwelling, green ones may live in trees, shrubs or grass and so on, while patterns consisting of blotches, saddles, bands or longitudinal stripes all help to break up the outline of the snake, especially when it is resting in an area of dappled light or among dead leaves and branches. For educational purposes, camouflaged snakes can be displayed on a substrate such as pine needles, leaves or bracken, when the effectiveness of their colours and markings becomes obvious (but note the remarks in Chapter 2 regarding substrate).

Another, more dramatic, characteristic is the ability of some snakes to produce venom and inject it into their prey (or predator) by forcing it through special grooved or tubular teeth, the fangs. It is probably this ability which has done so much harm to the reputation of all snakes but which is also, paradoxically, partially responsible for their popularity as 'pets'. Both attitudes, however, are wrong; only a small minority of species are dangerously venomous to humans, and even these are harmless if left in peace, while the motive for keeping snakes in captivity should be a genuine interest in them as animals rather than a personal leaning towards exhibitionism.

In common with other reptiles, snakes are covered in scales which help to protect them from dehydration when living in dry environments. Like other reptiles, too, they are incapable of producing their own body heat, as do birds and mammals, and must therefore rely on outside sources, e.g. the sun. Since they operate most efficiently at about 25–30°C (77–86°F), it follows that they are most abundant in the warmer parts of the world, especially the tropics and deserts, and are relatively scarce in cooler regions which have a winter each year. Those which have adapted to slightly less than ideal climates exhibit modified behaviour patterns which enable them to exploit what little heat there is and at the same time protect themselves from lethally cold temperatures. These strategies include hibernation during the winter; activity during the day (most tropical species are nocturnal); basking in a warm place; small size; dark coloration; and giving birth to living young, having retained their eggs in their body where the temperature can be controlled by moving about. All these species are usually referred to as 'temperate' as opposed to 'tropical'.

An understanding of the importance of thermoregulation is absolutely essential if snakes are to thrive in captivity. They do not just 'like' to be warm, they *must* be warm in order for the various chemical reactions which control their body functions to take place. These include such

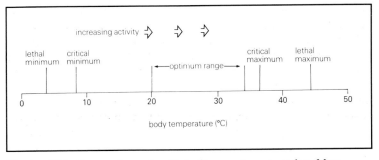

Fig. 1.   This diagram shows the effect of temperature on snakes. Most species operate most efficiently between 25 and 30°C (77 and 86°F) but will survive at temperatures above and below this.

fundamental activities as locomotion, digestion and spermatogenesis. The snake's body may be likened to a machine which is operated by a temperature-controlled battery; as the temperature drops, the battery gradually fades and one by one all the workings of the machine run down. By the same token, if the temperature exceeds certain limits this will also cause the machine to malfunction. The snake keeps its 'battery' at the correct temperature by exposing and aligning its body to the sun if it is too cold, and moving into the shade if it is too hot. When it is unable to maintain the 'preferred' temperature, for instance in the evening in cool climates, it finds a place where it will not be vulnerable to predators while it is helpless. Similarly, temperate species seek out underground hiding places in the autumn where they can retreat down to a level where they will be protected from lethal winter temperatures. If captive snakes are to lead a normal life, some provision must be made to ensure that they are able to maintain their bodies at suitable temperatures at the appropriate times of the year (see Fig. 1). This important aspect is discussed more fully in Chapter 2.

Another aspect of snakes' biology which sets them apart from most other animals is the fact that, not only are they all carnivorous, but they must also eat their food whole. Furthermore, most species are fairly specific in their food requirements and may only eat one type of prey. Therefore, a reliable food supply, of a type which is sometimes not easily available, must be assured before they are obtained. This may involve breeding food animals, a task which can be time-consuming and expensive, and it is also an important consideration when choosing which species to keep.

On the subject of health, few veterinarians are experienced in the treatment of reptilian diseases; indeed, there is still a great deal to learn about the natural history of these diseases and the way in which they affect snakes. This means that great care must be taken in choosing healthy animals at the outset and in ensuring that disease is not introduced via new acquisitions, food, etc. There are no inoculations against snake diseases and no simple, reliable treatments against many of them.

These remarks are not intended to dampen the enthusiasm of the beginner, but rather to point out that keeping and breeding snakes can be a challenge. Because of this, the sense of achievement that goes with successfully keeping and breeding one of the more difficult species is far greater than can ever be experienced with domestic pets. Many amateur herpetologists have made significant contributions to the understanding of snakes' natural history, and aspects of breeding, feeding, longevity and so on can only be fully investigated through the expertise of snake-keepers.

CHAPTER 2

Housing

Of necessity, snake cages are usually designed and built by the snake-keeper; there is no universal cage which suits every species or situation and consequently little incentive for commercial models to be developed. However, this need not be a drawback because a home-built cage can be designed and built to suit every need and every pocket. A number of suggested designs are given, each flexible as regards size, and suitable for a number of purposes.

The main considerations in cage design are that the cage should be escape-proof and capable of providing a correct, and preferably adjustable, environment. Environmental factors to be considered are heat, light and ventilation. Whereas these parameters will be dealt with in Chapter 3, it should be noted that all of them, and especially humidity, will be dependent to some extent on the basic design.

The size of cage required for a particular snake depends not only on the size of the snake, but also on its behaviour. Most snakes which are commonly kept are rather inactive and spend much time coiled up out of sight, but others are fast-moving and active, and these will require proportionately larger cages or they will invariably suffer damage to their snouts through impact with the sides. Having said this, it is true that snakes are quite content with, and may even prefer, small cages. After all, under natural conditions many of them spend most of their time hidden in a hollow log or beneath the ground and move about only to look for food or a mate. As a rule of thumb, one square foot of usable floor space per foot of snake is sufficient for species such as kingsnakes, ratsnakes, boas and pythons, but up to double this for active kinds such as whipsnakes and racers. Garter snakes and water snakes fall about midway between these two extremes, i.e. $1\frac{1}{2}$ square feet per foot of snake. Snakes sharing a cage also share all of the available space, in other words, each can make use of almost as much area as if it had the cage to itself.

Therefore, two, three or even four snakes living together need a cage the same size, or perhaps only slightly larger, than that required by the largest individual (although 'communities' of snakes living together can create other problems and are, if possible, best avoided).

The most usual shape for a snake cage is rectangular, with the length, width and height being in the proportions 2:1:1, but there is no reason why they should not be square or even triangular. Long, narrow cages are best avoided, however, as are complicated shapes which could make servicing difficult. Since most of the species which are kept are ground-dwelling, the height of their cage is not critical, 30 cm (12 in) usually being sufficient for snakes up to about 1 m (3 ft) in length; but a few species which are available from time to time, for instance green snakes (*Opheodryas*), some ratsnakes (*Elaphe*), and some boas and pythons, are partially arboreal and appreciate branches on which to climb, and so their cages must obviously be high enough to accommodate these.

(i) Aquarium type cage

Glass aquariums are possibly the most widely used containers for snakes, although, in many cases, not necessarily the best. It is not too important whether they are constructed entirely of glass using silicon cement, or whether they have a frame of some sort. In either case, a lid will have to be devised.

In its most simple form this consists of a wooden or metal frame, covered with a mesh of nylon or metal gauze, or perforated metal or plastic sheeting. This must fit tightly enough to prevent the snake from escaping. It is better to use a number of clips than to rely on the lid's own weight to hold it in place, as snakes are experts at working their snouts into the slightest crack and then forcing their bodies through, and almost everyone who has kept snakes, myself included, will have experienced the 'empty cage syndrome'. If necessary, a light fitting can be incorporated into the lid.

Advantages of this type of cage are that it is readily available, only the lid needing special preparation; it gives good visibility (on all four sides, if necessary); and it can be easily and thoroughly washed and disinfected. Disadvantages are that it will be heavy and easily broken; it will not retain heat well; and ventilation will be from the top only, which is far from ideal since carbon dioxide and other gaseous waste products are heavier than air and will form a layer at the bottom – precisely where the snakes are living. The situation can be improved by replacing the glass back and/or sides of the aquarium with wood or plastic, into which a panel of gauze can be incorporated.

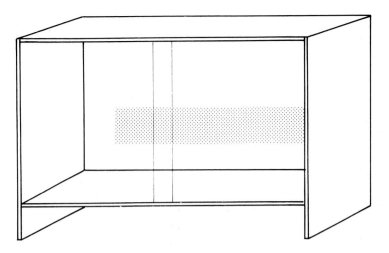

Fig. 2. A simple snake cage. The sides, base and top are of varnished or plastic-laminated wood, the back is of plastic-faced fibreboard and the front consists of two pieces of sliding glass. Note the ventilation panel in the back – large and positioned close to the bottom.

(ii) Glass-fronted cage

The most simple home-built snake cage is a wooden-carcassed box with a sliding glass front (*see* Fig. 2). The base, sides and top are made from boards about 6 mm ($\frac{1}{2}$ in) thick, preferably plastic-coated. Care must be taken to ensure that this construction is rigid and perfectly square, otherwise the glass front will not fit properly and will either stick or, worse, leave gaps through which the snakes will escape. For the same reason, if the cage is long, or if a rock or heavy water bowl is to be placed on the floor of the cage, extra support will be necessary in this region to prevent the base from bowing. In order to reduce weight, the back may be of plastic-faced hardboard, tacked to the carcass, and this should be generously drilled with holes, or a panel of perforated material incorporated. The inner joints of the wooden carcass may be sealed with aquarium sealant to allow thorough cleaning of the cage.

The sliding glass front can be arranged in two ways: it can slide up; or two pieces can be arranged to slide back on one another. Upward-sliding glass, which is really only suitable for small cages, is held in a single-channel plastic strip, glued or nailed to the sides of the cage. In order for it to clear the top, this must either be recessed or the channel must be angled slightly (*see* Fig. 3). Similarly, it must be angled if the cages are to be stacked on top of each other. Great care must be taken with these cages to ensure that the glass is held up securely (or removed altogether)

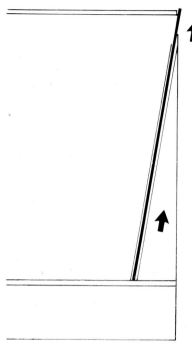

Fig. 3. An arrangement using a single upward-sliding glass cage front which enables cages to be stacked on top of each other. Single pieces of glass are only suitable for small cages and should be firmly wedged or removed completely while the cage is serviced.

while the cage is serviced, otherwise it acts rather like a guillotine! A horizontally sliding glass front is fitted by using double-channel plastic strip fixed to the roof and floor of the cage (noting that the top channel is deeper than the bottom to allow the glass to be lifted in and out). The two pieces of glass should overlap slightly when closed, and if very small snakes (or pregnant females belonging to live-bearing species) are to be housed in this way, a strip of foam must be stuck to the edge of one of the pieces in order to prevent escapes (although, strictly speaking, such species are more safely housed in other types of cage). Small wedges can be used to prevent the cages from opening accidentally (*see* Fig. 4) or, better still, special locks of the types used in showcases can be fitted – this is absolutely essential if venomous species are being kept. If wood shavings, bark chippings or other loose materials are used as a substrate, a small ledge positioned behind the glass will prevent this from falling into the bottom channel; alternatively, the channel itself may be raised an inch or two by fitting a lip inside the front of the cage.

Lighting and heating equipment is easily fitted to the lid or sides of this type of cage, as are branches, hide-boxes, etc. Such cages can also be conveniently stacked, especially if angled metal is fixed to the tops for slotting in the next tier, making them more economical on space than

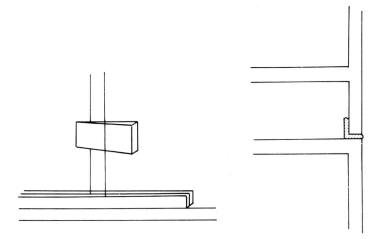

Fig. 4. Two pieces of sliding glass can be fixed with small rubber or wooden wedges to prevent the snakes from opening the cage. Cages containing poisonous snakes should be locked.

Fig. 5. If cages are to be stacked on top of each other it is recommended that strips of angled metal are used to prevent them from slipping apart.

aquaria, which must be serviced from the top (*see* Fig. 5). Several snakes can be kept in a large unit subdivided into individual chambers with fixed or removable partitions 'condominium-style', but there are problems associated with this design, especially those of ventilation and the risk of cross-infection. A number of single interlocking units, although more expensive to construct, will create a more versatile system.

(iii) Glass-fronted type with drawer

Really a development of the previous cage, drawer-type cages have been used successfully for keeping and breeding a variety of secretive snakes. Basically, a wooden cage is built with a false floor, beneath which a removable drawer is fitted (Plate 1). A hole in the false floor gives access to the drawer, allowing the snakes to 'go underground' at will. In this way the main part of the cage can be serviced without disturbing the animals, food for one snake can be placed in the drawer while another is fed above, or a suitable substrate for egg-laying can be placed in the drawer. If wood-shavings, etc. are to be used as the substrate in the upper compartment, a short section of tubing fitted into the hole will form a lip and prevent this from falling into the drawer (*see* Fig. 6). This piece of tube

19

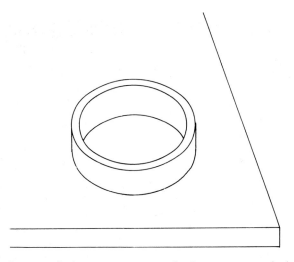

Fig. 6. Access to the lower compartment of a drawer-type cage is through a short section of plastic tube fitted into the false floor. It must not protrude below the floor.

must not be allowed to protrude beneath the false floor, otherwise it will prevent the complete removal of the drawer, and for equally obvious reasons, it is vital to ensure that snakes are not entering or leaving the drawer when this is pulled out! It will be necessary as well to obtain an appropriate number of plugs to prevent the snakes from moving in and out of the drawer during certain operations.

The most obvious drawback to this type of cage is the skill required to construct it with the necessary degree of accuracy, especially where the fit of the drawer is concerned. A neat solution is to use ready-made 'drawers' in the form of plastic bowls, such as washing-up bowls, which are available in a variety of sizes. The dimensions of the main part of the cage are then arranged to accommodate these. Additional advantages are that the bowls are easily washed or replaced if soiled, and that two or more small bowls may be placed under a single cage, with a hole leading to each, making it possible to isolate several snakes for feeding, etc., or, for example, to place wood-shavings in one and moss for egg-laying in the other.

(iv) Special display cages

If neatly built, there is no reason why any of the above cages cannot be attractive. However, under certain circumstances it may be desirable to design a cage specifically for display purposes, while not overlooking the

1. A bank of drawer-type cages used for breeding colubrids by Robert Applegate.

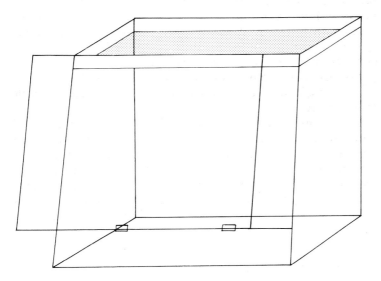

Fig. 7. A simply-built all-glass cage which forms an effective display for arboreal snakes. The same design can be applied to other sizes and shapes to simulate variety of habitats.

2. A rack designed to hold the maximum number of small lunch or shoe boxes. The snakes are prevented from opening the lids by the close fit of the boxes, and heating is by use of a heat-tape which runs along the back of each shelf, and can be seen looping from shelf to shelf on the side of the rack. This arrangement is ideal for rearing large numbers of young snakes.

requirements of the snakes, which must be of paramount importance. In addition, certain species have requirements which cannot be met by the rectangular 'shoe-box' shape and here it will also be necessary to be inventive. The tall glass cage illustrated in Fig. 7 is just one example of a design which has proved successful in housing unusual snakes, in this case the tropical arboreal species, *Sibon* and *Dipsas*, two snail-eating snakes. The diagram is more or less self-explanatory, but points to note are that the base section must be waterproof if water or very damp material is used in order to maintain a high humidity, and that the front panel should be securely clipped to the top 'rail'. Access to the cage is achieved by removing the front completely (for cleaning, etc.) or by lifting the perforated ventilation panel (for feeding or spraying). Provided that this cage is well ventilated and lit, it can be used to grow a variety of robust tropical plants, preferably types which do not require soil, such as bromeliads and epiphytic ferns. Alternatively, plants may be grown in pots using inert substances such as pebbles or 'Hortag' (horticultural clay beads) to cover the exposed soil in the pot. Obviously, this cage, and others like it, can be modified to cater for a range of habitat types.

(v) Plastic boxes

Many serious snake-breeders use opaque plastic or polythene boxes for rearing young snakes or for housing their breeding stock. These are

3. Texas Thread Snake, *Leptotyphlops dulcis*, a primitive burrowing snake, suitable only for the specialist. It requires a small box with a good layer of damp soil, and a diet of termites or small crickets.

readily available in a variety of sizes as lunch boxes, food storage boxes or, in the United States, as shoe or sweater boxes. Their great advantages are that they are cheap, easily cleaned and may be purchased as and when required. The only necessity is to cut openings in the lid and possibly in the sides, and 'weld' pieces of gauze over these openings. Of course, if opaque or translucent polythene boxes are used, the snakes cannot readily be seen without removing the lid, but if breeding is the main objective, this limitation is perfectly acceptable. Indeed, the snakes will prefer the security and diffuse lighting which they receive. Such a cage cannot be heated individually, but this need not be a drawback if a large number are to be used as they may be conveniently accommodated on a heated rack or shelf system as described in Chapter 3 (Plate 2). Even where a snake collection is maintained primarily for display purposes, animals may be housed in these boxes temporarily during their period of hibernation or cooling off during the winter, when receiving veterinary treatment or during quarantine. This type of 'cage' is also perfect for keeping small burrowing snakes such as the worm and thread snakes, *Typhlopidae* and *Leptotyphlopidae*, which require small containers and 5–8 cm (2–3 in) of moist, crumbly substrate in which to live (Plate 3).

CHAPTER 3

The Right Environment

This chapter is devoted to the environmental requirements of captive snakes. Although the exact values of temperature, light and humidity differ slightly from species to species, it is useful to obtain some general information on these parameters and how they may best be met. The most important consideration is that the snakes 'feel' right. Unfortunately for them, they will often tolerate conditions which are far from perfect, but any deviation from the conditions to which they have adapted throughout the course of their evolution is bound to create stress, and *stress is the single most important cause of disease, failure to eat and failure to breed.* Any natural environment consists of an interplay of a great many factors, and in order to create a good artificial environment it is necessary to unravel the most relevant of these and deal with each in turn. The factors with which we are concerned are, in order of importance, heat, light and humidity. Connected with these is another, less obvious, but also important factor – security. Whereas it is true that some species and some individuals are less shy and retiring than others, it is essential to realise that snakes are not, by nature, 'showy' animals, and if it is the intention to display animals which will be colourful and active all of the time, tropical fish or parrots would be a better choice.

As discussed in Chapter 1, temperature control is vitally important to snakes because they are unable to regulate their own body temperatures except by moving from a cool position to a warm one and vice versa. In a cage, the opportunities for this will obviously be limited to a fairly small range and so it is important to ensure that this is suitable. As a rule, snakes are most active at around 25–30°C (77–86°F). Tropical species should be maintained at this temperature at all times, although a slight drop at night will not be harmful. Temperate species should also be kept at this temperature during the day but a drop to 15–20°C (59–68°F) at night is more appropriate. Generally speaking, tropical species, such as boas, are far more susceptible to temperature fluctuations than are temperate ones, and so require more attention in respect of temperature control. Basically, each species of snake can tolerate a certain temperature range, outside of which it will not feed and may become vulnerable to disease. Species which experience a wide range of temperatures in nature will be better equipped to thrive under these conditions, while tropical species which are not naturally susceptible to great fluctuations are therefore less adaptable. However, the optimum temperature only needs to be maintained in one part of the cage: if a thermal gradient is created, the snakes will have the option of being warm or cool, and this is a perfectly natural arrangement. If facilities are such that a steady temperature cannot be provided, it is advisable to steer clear of the more demanding species.

During autumn, it may be found that a combination of cool nights and shortening days causes some snakes to stop feeding. If this occurs, a decision must be made whether or not to hibernate them. This involves lowering the daytime temperature, or moving the snakes to a cooler place, gradually bringing them down to 10–15°C (50–59°F) when activity will almost cease and they will remain in their hide-box most of the time. Drinking water must be provided, however, and small specimens, such as baby garter snakes, should be lightly sprayed with water from time to time to prevent dehydration. If the decision is to keep them active throughout the winter (in order to grow young specimens on as quickly as possible, for instance), they may be treated as for tropical species; but sometimes an individual will refuse food during its natural hibernation period despite a warm environment, and therefore must be kept cool in order to prevent its food reserves from being used up prematurely. (This is often the case with wild-caught individuals during their first, and sometimes subsequent winters, and certain species are more or less obligate hibernators, *Lampropeltis pyromelana* being an example.)

It must also be realised that many species are reluctant to breed unless they have been 'cooled off' for a period of two to three months in the winter – this is discussed in more detail in Chapter 6.

Those snake-keepers who live in the warmer parts of the world may be able to dispense with artificial heating altogether. Elsewhere, however, some means of providing the correct temperature for the animals must be devised. To some extent, the type of heating equipment used will depend on the design of cage in use and also on the number of cages which house the collection. For many years, traditional means of heating reptiles has been to rely entirely on a light bulb of appropriate wattage in each cage. This provides light and heat at the same time and may be suitable for some snakes. The disadvantage is that heat cannot be provided *without* light, and vice versa, and this is not always desirable. A better arrangement is to provide a suitable background temperature by some other means, perhaps using small light bulbs to boost the heating slightly during the day. Furthermore, for certain types of cages, notably the afore-mentioned plastic boxes, the fitting of light bulbs is totally impractical, and alternative means of heating must be used. One method is to heat the room in which the collection is housed, but this presupposes that every species kept requires the same temperature, and all that can be done to deal with this problem is to vary the level at which the several cages are stored. A better method, developed during the last few years, is to use bottom heat in the form of heat tapes, heat cables or heat pads. None of these devices have been produced for the purpose of heating snake cages; heat tapes are designed to coil around pipes to prevent them from freezing, while heat cables and heat pads are intended for use in the horticultural world, as a means of accelerating seed germination and plant growth. Heat tapes are more readily available, and therefore more widely used, in the United States than in Europe, but the principle of all these items is the same; and as a rule, they can be obtained in a range of sizes and power ratings. Whereas the tapes and cables can be adapted to heat a number of cages, heat pads are normally used for heating individual cages. They may be placed beneath the cage or inside it and should be arranged so that their effect is localised in one area, allowing the occupants of the cage to move from warm to cool areas.

Heat tapes and cables are most commonly installed on the shelf or shelves on which the cages rest (see Fig. 8). They may be rebated into the shelf itself or placed on the surface, in which case the cages can be raised slightly by fixing thin strips of wood to the front and back of the shelf. If plastic cages are to be used, direct contact with the heating element must be avoided due to the risk of fire, and it may also be necessary to place a sheet of thin metal over the shelf in order to dissipate the heat – because the efficiency of the equipment varies from one brand to another, as will the background temperature, this will require some experimentation. Note also that the cages to be heated need not necessarily all be on the same shelf; the tape or cable can be arranged to pass from one shelf to the one above or below, the only precaution being to ensure that it can be removed and replaced should it prove to be faulty or of the wrong power output. One way in which this can be done is illustrated in Fig. 9.

In order to provide the thermal gradient which is necessary for snakes to thrive, the tape or cable must be arranged towards the front or, preferably, the back of the shelf. All sorts of variations are possible with this basic arrangement. For example, two elements (of either type) may be combined, with or without thermostats, to control the temperature within narrow limits. One will provide the night-time temperature and will be set fairly low, say 20°C (68°F) – this will be connected to the power

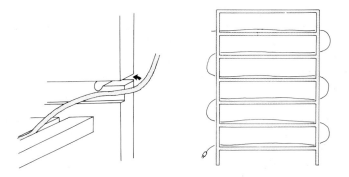

Fig. 8. (*Above left*) The back of a shelf, recessed to house a heating cable. In order to remove and replace the cable, the sides of the rack are notched as shown, and if two or more cables are to be installed further notches will be necessary, although weakening the structure must be avoided.

Fig. 9. (*Above right*) A single tape or cable can be used to heat a number of cages on a free-standing rack or shelf unit.

Fig. 10. A suggested arrangement for providing a temperature rise during the day. One heat tape or cable is linked to a time-switch which can also operate the lights if necessary. The other is left on permanently and provides background heat.

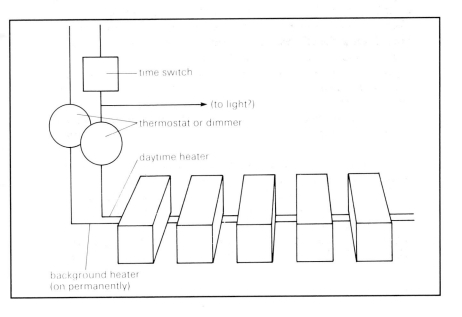

at all times – while the other will provide a boost to say 25°C (77°F) during the day and will be controlled via a time-switch which can also operate the lights. By altering the on-off settings throughout the year, a consistent daily and seasonal rhythm can be reproduced (*see* Fig. 10). By observing the behaviour of the snakes it should be possible to reach the correct temperature for every species which is kept. If the temperature is too high, the snakes will be found as far away from the heat as possible at all times, in which case the output may be reduced by means of a rheostat (i.e. a dimmer), the cages may be raised slightly on wood or styrofoam sheets, or they can be pulled forward on the shelf. If several species are housed on the same shelf and there are obvious differences in such behavioural patterns, either of the two latter suggestions is the best course of action, but if all the snakes are behaving in the same way, adjustment of the output is simpler. If, on the other hand, they spend nearly all of their time resting over the heat source, the likelihood is that they are being kept too cool and the heat should be increased, if necessary by adding a second tape or cable. The ideal situation is where the snakes are seen to be actively regulating their body temperatures by moving back and forth within the cage, spending more time over the heat source just after they have eaten, when they are about to shed their skins or if they contain developing eggs or young, but being randomly distributed at all other times.

LIGHTING

As far as the more common snakes are concerned, artificial lighting is probably more important to the keeper than to the kept. Most snakes prefer subdued lighting, many of them being nocturnal by nature or active during the early morning/late evening periods, and the incidental light entering their cages via windows is normally sufficient. However, in cages which are kept on display, or those kept in windowless rooms, some form of lighting is usually called for, and here fluorescent lamps are the items of choice, being economical to run and producing a minimum of heat. A variety of different colour-balanced tubes are available, including those that enhance colour, e.g. 'Gro-lux', and others which approximate to a normal spectrum, e.g. 'Vita-lite' and 'Tru-lite'. But since most snakes will not benefit greatly from the light anyway, the choice of type is of little importance, except that high intensities should be avoided.

Nevertheless, there may be circumstances under which the quality of light *is* important. Certain snakes which habitually bask in the sun may require light, either for psychological reasons or in order to metabolise. (It is well known that many species of lizards use sunlight to produce

4. Auxiliary equipment for the snake cage: a ceramic heater with reflector, for creating a hot-spot in the cage; a spotlight which provides ultra-violet as well as visible light: and a heating pad, designed to be buried in the substrate.

Vitamin D, and will not survive unless it, or a suitable substitute, is provided; and some snakes, such as the whipsnakes and racers, which have a similar life-style to these lizards may have the same requirement.) It may also be thought desirable, occasionally, to include living plants in a snake's cage: they, too, have light requirements that must be met if they are to survive, although obviously these must not conflict with the best interests of the snake. Details of suitable lighting equipment are easily obtainable from the horticultural literature.

In individual cages, it is usually simplest to mount the tube(s) inside the cage, using metal clips attached to the top, with the starter unit outside, but if cages are arranged along a shelf there may be sufficient room to fix self-contained units to the underside of the shelf above. The lights may be switched on and off by hand, but a time-switch incorporated into the circuit is usually more convenient (Plate 4).

Temperate species experience a seasonal fluctuation in light levels and day-length as well as in temperature. If it is wished to simulate natural conditions as closely as possible, this must obviously be taken into account and the day-length varied from 8 hours in the winter to 16 hours at the height of summer, usually being increased and decreased by about one hour at a time throughout the year. Owing to their secretive habits, however, it is unlikely that day-length is as important to snakes as is temperature in stimulating breeding activity. Tropical species would normally experience little or no change in day-length and it is as well to retain a year-round 12:12 light cycle for them.

HUMIDITY

Accurate control of humidity is not usually important, but most species do better if it is kept low at all times. This simply involves ensuring that the cage is well ventilated – the cage heating will then drive off excess moisture, leading to a dry atmosphere and dry substrate, the latter being especially important. If the snakes require more moisture, as they sometimes do immediately prior to shedding their skin, they will normally obtain this by coiling up in the water container. Certain tropical rain-forest species (which are rarely kept) require more humid conditions, otherwise they regularly encounter problems in shedding their skins, and here it may be necessary to spray the cage daily in order to achieve this. Note that good ventilation is still vital – no snakes enjoy a damp, stagnant atmosphere and only a few require a permanently damp substrate. An alternative method of creating the right degree of humidity, especially for arboreal rain-forest species such as some of the pit-vipers (e.g. *Trimeresurus* sp.), is to place a false floor of perforated plastic in their cage and maintain 5–8 cm (2–3 in) of heated water beneath this, causing a constant current of moist air to pass up through the cage and out of the ventilation panels.

CAGE FURNISHINGS

The substrate of a snake's cage must meet three main requirements: it must be dry, non-toxic and easily cleaned or replaced. In practice, this leaves a relatively small number of suitable materials. Newspaper, though not particularly attractive, is cheap and easily obtained, and is no trouble to replace every time it becomes soiled. Several layers should be cut or folded to size, and it may be necessary to tape the edges to prevent the snakes from living permanently beneath it. If required, it can be disguised to some extent by a layer of dry pine needles, bracken or dead leaves.

Wood-shavings are a rather more pleasant alternative. They should be of white wood (because certain red woods contain plant toxins which may have harmful side-effects), free from dust, and come from untreated timber – shavings sold as bedding for small mammals are ideal. A fairly thick layer should be used, and it may be advantageous to place a layer of newspaper beneath it.

Bark chippings are possibly the most attractive of the easily available substrates and are suitable for the larger species of snakes, but have the disadvantage of being expensive; since they cannot be washed, regular changes are necessary and this adds substantially to maintenance costs.

Materials to be avoided are soil, sharp sand and fine gravel, all of which become damp, tend to harbour pests and parasites, and may physically damage snakes, especially if accidentally swallowed along with food. However, exceptions to this rule may have to be made in the case of certain burrowing snakes. Some of these, for example, the sand boas, genus *Eryx*, and desert colubrids such as the shovel-nosed snakes, *Chionactis*, fare better if kept in a substrate of dry sand – not sharp (e.g. builders') sand, but horticultural silver sand, which has rounded particles. In addition, small burrowing snakes, such as worm and thread snakes, require a substrate of moist (*not* waterlogged), crumbly material such as leaf-mould, decayed wood or chopped moss.

It hardly needs to be said that snakes which are totally aquatic must be kept in water, but this applies to a very limited number of species, notably the fishing snake, *Erpeton tentaculatum*, and its relatives, and the wart, or elephant trunk snakes, *Acrochordidae*. It does *not* apply to many other so-called 'water' snakes such as members of the genera *Nerodia* from North America or *Natrix* from Europe and Asia, nor to garter snakes, genus *Thamnophis*. These species, although naturally inhabitants of swamps and other damp habitats, are especially prone to skin conditions that result from perpetual contact with a damp substrate; so it is imperative that they are kept on one of the dry substrates listed at the beginning of this section, and that their amphibious tendencies are restricted to a small water bowl.

Apart from substrate, other cage furnishings should be kept to a minimum. A water bowl is essential, and should be of glazed stoneware or plastic in order to facilitate thorough cleaning. It should be heavy and stable in order to prevent tipping and, if it is large enough for a snake to crawl into, it should be kept less than half full so that it does not overflow – all these measures are aimed at keeping the substrate dry. A novel water bowl, designed for use with small snakes was shown to me recently and is illustrated in Fig. 11. It consists of a small plastic food container, complete with lid, into which is cut a small circular opening

Fig. 11. A novel type of water bowl which will not spill water if the snake tips it over. It is made from a plastic food container with a circular hole cut in the lid. Snakes, especially young ones, appear to prefer to soak in this type of bowl than in a completely open one.

which provides access for the snake. Less than 1 cm ($\frac{1}{2}$ in) of water is contained, and so the lid prevents spillage even if the bowl is tipped onto its side. In addition, the snakes appear to like the security of the bowl and benefit from soaking in it before shedding. Unless a drawer is incorporated into the cage, a hide-box is a necessity for most snakes. This consists of a small container with an opening just large enough for the snake to enter. A cardboard box with a small hole cut in one side makes an adequate hide-box, and one which can easily be replaced if soiled or damaged. A more permanent item can be made of plywood, varnished and sealed inside so that it can be wiped clean, or a plastic box can be adapted.

An inverted clay flower-pot makes a good improvised hide-box and snakes soon learn to gain access through the drainage hole; and for arboreal snakes such as some young boas, a wicker nest basket, as used for breeding cage birds, can be lodged or hung near the top of the cage. Apart from providing a secure place in which to rest, hide-boxes can be useful for feeding snakes which are reluctant to feed out in the open and, if a door or bung is available, can be used to separate individuals during feeding, etc. Hide-boxes are also valuable for removing nervous, aggressive or venomous snakes from their cages while these are being serviced, for transferring them from one cage to another, or for placing them in a cool room during hibernation.

Although these three items – floor-covering, water bowl and hide-box – are the only real essentials in a snake cage, many keepers like to add one or two natural items to enhance the appearance of their cages. Logs and branches are better than rocks because they are lighter and make a more pleasing arrangement, and they may be essential if arboreal snakes are kept. Branches should be firmly wedged or fixed to the sides or top of the cage, and should obviously be strong enough to carry the weight of the snakes. If parasite infestations occur, the branches should be discarded and replaced, and it is a good idea to do this as a matter of course when changing the occupants of the cage. There is no reason why plastic plants should not be included for effect, but the snakes will be indifferent! However, there may be a case for including live plants under certain circumstances, since they are important indicators of light and humidity. The plants selected should ideally originate from the same region and habitat as the snakes, and because of the problems associated with using soil in a cage are best chosen from among the various epiphytic species which are available. These include a wide range of bromeliads (air plants), that require varying degrees of humidity and heat, ferns such as *Asplenium nidus*, and a large number of epiphytic orchids. By providing conditions that are suitable for the plants, it should be possible to maintain successfully any of the snake species which are associated with them in nature, but this logic does not always apply and caution should be exercised. Plants may also be used to demonstrate natural biotopes which includes snakes, but this is usually done on a much more ambitious scale than the average snake-keeper would wish to attempt, and is beyond the scope of this book.

CHAPTER 4

Health and Management

MANAGEMENT

Day-to-day management of a snake collection is much like looking after other animals. Certain routine tasks must be carried out regularly and additional time should be spent observing the animals – only by getting to know what is 'normal' behaviour for an individual is it possible to spot something amiss before it is too late. In other words, the animals should be looked in on *every day*, even if it is only to say hello!

Faeces, shed skins and uneaten food should be removed as soon as they are seen and not left until a 'cleaning-out day' comes around. All waste should be discarded straight away and not be allowed to lie around in a waste bin in the animal room. A spoon or scoop may be used for removing faeces and contaminated bedding, and if all of the animals are fed on the same day this task is usually necessary four to five days later. If this is not the case, something could be wrong (although there will always be some variation), so check the temperature of the cage and keep a close eye on the snake for abnormal behaviour.

Water bowls should be emptied, rinsed and replenished every other day and now and then each cage should be completely cleaned out, washed or wiped with a disinfectant such as a 3–5% solution of sodium hypochlorite (domestic bleach) and rinsed. Water bowls should be similarly treated, and soiled branches, rocks and hide-boxes either replaced or thoroughly scrubbed and disinfected. The exact period over which this will be necessary will depend on the size of the snake, its diet, the dimensions of the cage, the effectiveness of the ventilation and the type of substrate in use – let your nose be your guide.

Unless you have absolute confidence in your craftsmanship, it is also a good idea to inspect any home-built cages occasionally for signs of warping, wear or general dilapidation; if you don't find the gaps, the snakes certainly will!

HEALTH

Wild snakes are normally a fairly healthy group of individuals. Whilst it is true that they carry their share of internal and external parasites, as do all animals, including humans, this rarely causes serious health problems unless the resistance of the snake becomes lowered through some form of stress.

Similarly, captive snakes are not normally prone to serious disorders unless they, too, are subjected to stress. This can be caused by an unsuitable environment, frequent handling (in the case of nervous species) and over-crowding. Poor hygiene can exacerbate the problem if faeces, scraps of shed skin, etc., are allowed to remain in the cage, providing a constant source of reinfection.

The most serious threat to the health of captive snakes, however, is contact with pathogens to which they have no resistance, i.e. by introducing wild-caught animals from different geographic regions or habitats. Often the keeper has little control over this if the animals are obtained from commercial sources, where reptiles from all four corners of the world are held in the same room – often in the same cage. A typical scenario is that animals are collected in, say, the Far East, and held in high densities prior to shipment. During this time the animals become stressed and their parasite and bacteria load soars. On arrival at their destination they are held in premises where other exotic species are also awaiting distribution. By the time the infected animals are sold, or die, their diseases will have been spread far and wide.

Problems of this sort can be avoided completely by purchasing only captive-bred animals from a reliable breeder. If this is not possible, then exotic animals bought from a dealer (even if the animals are kept impeccably) must be quarantined.

Quarantine involves housing the newly acquired animal(s) well away from established stock, preferably in a separate room. Feeding, cage-cleaning, etc. of quarantined animals must be left until after all others have been attended to, and all implements used (e.g. scoops, tongs, etc.) should be kept separately and ideally sterilised in a strong solution of bleach immediately after use. The new animals should be carefully watched for signs of disease and, in particular, their faeces should be examined for signs of infection; bad smell, fluid consistency, sometimes a greenish colour and visible parasites such as round worms (nematodes). If in doubt, send samples away for laboratory examination (through your vet.). Many keepers like to 'assume' that their new acquisition is sick and give a prophylactic course of antibiotics during the quarantine period, but indiscriminate dosing with powerful drugs is to be avoided.

The only other source of infection to established snakes kept in a closed colony (i.e. one in which new animals are not introduced) is through their food. There is really no reason for this to happen in the case of rodent-eating snakes since laboratory-bred stock, free from parasites, is as a rule readily available and there is no excuse for scraping dead animals off the road, for instance, in order to provide food for the snakes. Species which feed only on amphibians or lizards can present something of a problem since neither of these are often available as captive-bred items. There is no easy solution to this quandary; deep-freezing the meal before it is fed may eliminate some of the parasites (assuming that the snake will take dead food), but usually it is only possible to rely on the snake's ability to tolerate a natural parasite burden.

DISEASE

Prevention is always better than cure and this is doubly so when cures are hard to come by. However, it is unrealistic to think that disease can be avoided altogether, even if every precaution is taken. The following list of ailments is a sample only, but includes those most frequently encountered. In many cases, recommendations regarding specific drugs and dose rates are purposely omitted. This is partly due to the fact that medical opinion is always changing and that improved cures are constantly being introduced, but mainly due to the conviction that those persons best qualified to administer such treatments will already have access to the necessary information. In my experience DIY veterinary treatment kills more animals than it cures.

Bacterial infections

'Pneumonia'. Various organisms can cause respiratory infections in snakes, the symptoms of which include wheezing, sneezing and excess mucus in the mouth and nostrils. In severe cases the nostrils may be completely blocked, and the two forks of the tongue may stick together when it is flicked out. This problem is often caused by an unsuitable environment, and moving the snake to a warm, draught-free, but well-ventilated cage may be sufficient, although some infections are persistent and can be lethal; they are also highly infectious, and thus infected snakes should be isolated immediately and veterinary advice sought. Tylosin, by intramuscular injection at the rate of 25 mg/kg body weight, or Oxytetracycline given orally at 50 mg/kg have been successfully used for the treatment of these diseases.

Pseudomonas infection. This bacterium is almost always found in small numbers, even in healthy snakes. Under certain conditions it can lead to a variety of distinct diseases: mouth rot, which attacks the tissue of the gums, causing a cheesy deposit, and in severe cases, prevents the snake from closing its mouth completely; ulceration of the skin; and a form of intestinal infection in which the lining of the posterior part of the digestive tract is attacked. The problem is that most of these conditions can also be caused by a wide variety of other organisms, and so unless laboratory screening is possible it is not easy to suggest courses of action. If *Pseudomonas* is definitely present, Gentomycin is probably the best drug to use, at the rate of 2.5 mg/kg body weight, as an intramuscular injection. Some forms of mouth rot can often be cleared up by irrigating the infected area with an aqueous solution of 25% sulphamethazine, and skin ulcers sometimes respond to treatment with iodophors such as 'Betadine'. These are applied directly to the infected site with a wad of cotton wool.

Salmonellosis. Various bacteria belonging to the *Salmonella* group may infect captive snakes, but do not invariably give rise to disease. Symptoms of severe infections include wet, greenish faeces. Many antibiotics, such as Tetracycline and Chloramphenicol, are effective should treatment be considered necessary. Note that this condition may be transferable to humans.

Parasite infestations

Several parasites may be found in association with snakes, and are classified as endo- or ecto-parasites according to whether they exist on the inside or outside of the host's body.

1. *Endo-parasites*

Gastro-enteritis. A devastating disease caused by the protozoan *Entamoeba invadens*; infected snakes usually die within thirty days if not treated. Symptoms include regurgitation of food or failure to eat, and white, slimy stools with more than normal asssociated fluid. The drugs Emtryl (150 mg/kg body weight) and Flagyl (250 mg/kg body weight) have been found to be effective, and apparently have no side-effects; so this is one case where prophylactic treatment may be considered, but expert advice is essential. Note that this organism is not the only cause of regurgitation, which can also be caused by too low temperatures, too large meals and the elimination of gut bacteria following a previous course of antibiotic treatment.

Nematodes (round-worms). Nematode worms rarely constitute a serious threat to health, although some are thought to burrow out of the intestinal tract where they normally live and migrate to other parts of the body, where they encyst. This may give rise to small lumps or blisters just beneath the surface of the skin or, in some cases, may affect the nervous system of the snake. They are simply eliminated (at least while residing in the gut) by the administration of piperazine citrate (e.g. dog and cat worming tablets), dissolved in water and force-fed to the snake at the rate of 5 mg/100 g of snake. The treatment should be carried out once a week for three weeks.

Stongyloides worms. Eggs of these small worms may occasionally be found in the faeces of infested snakes, having been voided from the intestinal tract where the adults live. Although small numbers of them are probably tolerable to the snakes, they are fairly easily eliminated, at least for a while, by the use of an aqueous solution of Thiabenzole at the rate of 15–20 mg/100 g of snake, administered into the oesophagus via a rubber tube and syringe.

2. Ecto-parasites

The only serious ecto-parasite to which snakes are susceptible is the snake-mite, *Ophionyssus natricis*. These live on the surface of the snake's skin, breed rapidly and may be seen as small round brown or black creatures, either moving over the scales or lodged around the eye. Heavy infestations lead to the snake's scales being 'dusted' with small white specks (the mites' droppings). Although the direct damage which they cause (by sucking the host's blood) is probably not very great, they may easily act as carriers of disease by moving from cage to cage. Although frequent and thorough cage cleaning and the immediate removal of any pieces of shed skin will keep them under control, their complete elimination is so easy that there is no excuse for such infestations. A small piece of 'Vapona' or other dichlorvos-containing pest strip is placed in a small perforated container (an old film canister is ideal) and suspended inside the cage. This should kill all existing mites within a day or two, but the procedure should be repeated one week later in order to 'mop up' any young mites which have hatched in the meantime. Beware that dichlorvos can have harmful side-effects to snakes (and humans) and may even be fatal in large doses. Therefore, the substance should not be left in the cage as a matter of course, nor should the treatment be carried out more frequently than is necessary. Once the mites have been completely eliminated, discard the strip.

Ticks are often found on snakes which have been captured from the wild. They are larger than mites, sometimes the same size as one of the snake's scales, and firmly attached. Some species are rounded when well fed and may be felt quite easily if the snake is allowed to glide through one's hands, but another kind, commonly seen on royal pythons, for instance, is cunningly disguised as a scale, being flattened in shape and chestnut brown in colour. Ticks may be removed by dabbing them with alcohol, then grasping them with forceps and carefully turning them over ('head over heels') in order to unhook their mouthparts. Failure to do so may result in leaving these behind, where they can cause local infection.

Wounds and injuries are commonly found on newly captured snakes, either as a result of rough handling during capture or through their continual efforts to escape from a poorly made cage, whereupon they will rub the scales off the front of their snouts. These wounds should be treated by dusting the exposed areas with sulphanilamide powder, obtainable from a veterinarian. Antibiotics, such as penicillin, may also be used but current opinion is that drugs such as these should only be employed where no other treatment will work, in order to minimise the risk of immune strains of bacteria evolving.

Skin blisters, often found on, but not restricted to, natricine snakes, may be caused by a substrate which is too damp, in which case they will often clear up spontaneously once conditions are corrected. However, sometimes these blisters are persistent and may develop into a type of scale rot, caused by a secondary *Pseudomonas* infection (*see* above), which can be very difficult to cure. Occasionally, the application of antiseptic solutions such as 'Pevadine', or of sulphonamide or antibiotic powders, may work, but the condition is best avoided by examining wild-caught snakes very carefully before purchase.

Skin sloughing (or shedding) usually takes place without complications, the whole skin coming away in one piece. Occasionally, however, the snake turns opaque as usual but then fails to slough during the next week, with the skin gradually becoming dry and wrinkled; alternatively, the skin is only partially sloughed, large patches of it remaining attached to the snake. In either case the best treatment is to place the snake in a cotton 'snake-bag' which is half full of moist sphagnum moss and put it in a warm place (say back in its cage). The moss serves to soak the skin and also to grip it as the snake crawls about in the bag, and nine times out of ten it will come away completely after a day or two. If not, it may be necessary to work away manually at the edge of the skin, starting around the mouth if this section is still attached, until it becomes free, and then gradually peel the skin off; this is normally accomplished by gripping the snake fairly tightly and allowing it to crawl through the hands (non-venomous species only, please). If the problem occurs each time the snake is due to slough, then it may be worth considering raising the humidity in the cage, either by occasional spraying or by increasing the diameter of the water dish. A fairly common problem associated with skin-shedding is the retention of the scales which cover the eyes, even though the rest of the skin comes away without any trouble. These may be removed by wrapping adhesive tape around the index finger with the sticky side outwards and then pressing firmly against the eye. It may be necessary to repeat this several times before the scale is finally freed. If this does not work it will be necessary to attempt to pick the scale off with a fingernail, but great care must be taken. Pointed forceps should not be used for this operation.

RECORD KEEPING

There seems to be a great deal of polarisation among snake-keepers when it comes to record keeping; some loathe it, whereas others wait impatiently for something interesting to happen so that they can record it. Despite individual inclinations, it is obviously important to keep up-to-date records giving at least basic information on each animal. These records will prove invaluable if the animal requires treatment from a veterinarian, or, for instance, if it is wished to compare previous breeding data. In addition, the information which accumulates over several years may be of interest to others when summarised and published in a society bulletin.

Although the actual design of the card, notebook page, etc. are not too important, certain information should be accurately and regularly recorded, and presented in a form which makes it easily accessible. As a guideline, the following headings should be listed:

Species and subspecies (especially important if the animal is the result of a mating between two different forms), and sex.

Date of birth (or purchase) and parents (or source).

Food taken, with dates.

Sloughing (with dates).

Treatment for disease, and outcome.

Size and/or weight, recorded at fairly regular intervals, but at least once each year, e.g. immediately before entering a cooling-off period.

Breeding details – date(s) mated, date of pre-laying slough, date of laying or birth, number of eggs or young, date of hatching of eggs (and temperature of incubation), size of young, food of young, miscellaneous observations.

Date and cause of death.

If necessary, a sketch of some characteristic marking on each snake can be made on the appropriate record card in order that it can be recognised. The cards should be kept together, with those for living animals in one box and those for dead or sold animals in another (in some cases, purchasers may like to make a copy of their snake's details).

HANDLING

Snakes should not be handled more than is necessary, and in particular, they should not be handled shortly after a meal or during the period immediately prior to shedding their skin.

Handling of tame, non-venomous species is simply achieved by grasping them firmly at mid-body and lifting them up. Large specimens should then be further supported by the other hand (Plate 5). Most species will coil at least part of their body around the hand or wrist, making the operation easy. Individuals which are not so tame may attempt to bite when first picked up but will usually quieten down once they are off the ground. If necessary, they can be grasped just behind the head with one hand while the other hand supports the body, but too strong a grip in this region can easily do damage. If snakes are to be moved any distance it is advisable to place them in a soft cotton 'snake-bag' which is securely tied at the top. This avoids the possibility of them rubbing their snouts in an attempt to get out. During cage-cleaning operations, etc., it is usually sufficient to place them temporarily in a bucket with a lid which can be clipped into place. Alternatively, if the hide-box can be closed by means of a sliding door or a bung, the snake can be persuaded into this and removed without any direct handling.

Venomous species, even if only mildly so, should be handled with great care, not only to reduce the risk of being bitten, but also to avoid damaging the snake.

5.   Method of holding a tame, non-venomous snake.

6.   (*Below left*) Using a snake hook to lift a small venomous snake out of its cage so that cleaning, etc. can take place.

7.   (*Below right*) A grab-stick, for handling fast-moving venomous species, and a pair of long tongs, used for offering food to venomous or arboreal snakes. Note the storage place – on the wall where they will not be a hazard should a venomous snake escape.

Vipers can usually be lifted out of their cage by means of a short snake hook which is eased under their body about half-way along (Plate 6). They can then be placed in a bucket or bin. If they are to be bagged up for transportation, the bag may either be placed over the rim of the bucket, or a special bag, with a series of press-studs arranged around the opening so that it can be fixed over the frame of a butterfly net, may be used. (*See* Fig. 12.) Once the snake is in the bottom of the bag, it is trapped there by holding a bar or pole across the bag while the top is unclipped and securely tied. It is important to hold the bag well away from the body as it is being carried since there is always a possibility that the snake will strike through the bag. Cobras, owing to their speed and agility, are not nearly so easy to handle. They will rarely allow themselves to be lifted on a snake hook nor can they be easily pinned down or held behind the head without risk of injury. Large specimens may be picked up with a grab-stick, a piece of apparatus consisting of a pole with a pair of metal or plastic jaws at one end and a handle at the other. The jaws are operated by means of a trigger located on the handle (Plate 7). In order to avoid damaging the snake, it is advisable to cover the jaws with rubber tubing or a layer of foam. Grab-sticks are available from some reptile dealers, but similar pieces of equipment are manufactured in order to enable elderly people to pick up objects without bending, and these can usually be easily adapted for snake-handling.

By far the best way of manipulating these animals is to incorporate a removable hide-box into their cage and arrange for this to be closed from

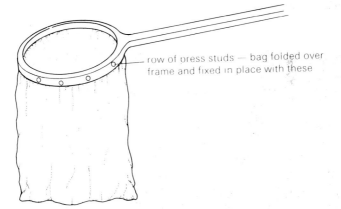

row of press studs — bag folded over frame and fixed in place with these

Fig. 12. A safe way of bagging a venomous snake consists of using the frame from a butterfly net to hold the bag open. This is attached to the frame by means of a series of press studs around the opening. Once the snake is an the bag it should be trapped in the bottom, using a bar or pole, while the bag is detached from the frame and securely tied.

outside the cage. Once they are safely incarcerated, the cage can be cleaned or the animal, complete with its box, can be removed.

Occasionally it is necessary to restrain venomous snakes in order to administer drugs, determine their sexes by probing, or remove pieces of unshed skin. A number of methods have been described in the literature, of which the most convenient and practicable are listed at the beginning of Chapter 12.

CHAPTER 5

Feeding

TYPES OF FOOD

All snakes are carnivorous, feeding on a wide variety of animals ranging from ants and termites up to large mammals. As they have no means of dismembering their prey, it must be swallowed whole. The size of the prey therefore depends on the size of the snake, although most species are able to increase their gape by temporarily dislocating the bones of their lower jaw as they engulf their food.

The preferred prey of the various species must be carefully considerd when choosing animals for captivity because some are very specialised and may only accept food which is not readily available, for instance, toads or lizards. In practice, the choice for most snake-keepers will be limited to species which eat invertebrates such as earthworms or insects, fish, birds (chicks), or small mammals such as mice and rats. However, a large number of species fall into this category and there should be no difficulty in finding something suitable.

The food listed above may be obtained in a number of ways. Earthworms can usually be collected at certain times of the year and may be kept alive by housing them in a wooden or polystyrene (styrofoam) box containing 15–23 cm (6–9 in) of soil mixed with a good quantity of dead leaves. If this is placed in a cool but frost-free place, the worms should stay alive, if necessary, for several months. There are several alternative ways of catering for fish-eating species. Small fish may be collected, purchased or bred. An easier solution, for those snakes that will accept it, is to buy frozen fish. These may be small whole fish such as sand-eels or larger pieces which must be cut into narrow strips (*see* Fig. 13). Each strip should contain some bone and some skin – the most convenient way of ensuring this is to buy small flatfish (dabs, flounders, etc.) and cut them transversely – each slice will then contain a section of the bone. However, snakes which are fed entirely on fish may develop a deficiency of Vitamin

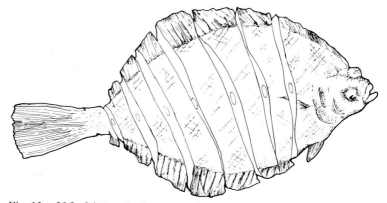

Fig. 13. If flatfish are sliced transversely, each strip will contain a small piece of bone which will provide calcium and phosphorus.

B1 (thiamin), due to the enzyme thiaminase present in the fish. This leads eventually to a disorder of the nervous system, making the snake lose muscle control. Apparently, only certain types of fish, e.g. oily fish such as whitebait, are responsible for this particular probem. It can be overcome by adding Vitamin B1 to the diet, achieved most conveniently by using a multivitamin powder, or by destroying the thiaminase before the fish is fed to the snakes. This is done by placing the strips of fish in water, and heating it to 80°C (47°F) for five minutes.

The majority of snakes offered for sale by breeders or dealers will be rodent-eaters. These include most of the boas and pythons, the ratsnakes and the kingsnakes. Depending on their size, it will be necessary to ensure a reliable supply of newborn mice (known as 'pinkies') for hatchling snakes, and adult mice or rats for larger specimens. In an emergency, small snakes will sometimes accept pieces of mouse, for instance a leg, if appropriately sized food is not available. If you have obtained your snake from a local dealer, he should also be prepared to supply its food, but it may be possible to breed mice and/or rats in order to guarantee a regular supply, but be warned, this can easily take up more space and time than the maintenance of your snakes, and the cost of producing food in this way often exceeds the cost of buying it, especially if only small quantities are involved. A compromise can sometimes be made by buying in all food for adult snakes, but keeping a small breeding nucleus of mice in order to obtain a steady supply of pinkies for the hatchlings. It is important to realise, though, that any live animals which are reared as snake food are entitled to the same degree of care as the snakes themselves, and there is no excuse for rearing or maintaining food animals under poor conditions.

Large species, especially pythons, will take day-old chicks, which may be obtained from a local poultry farm or from a reptile dealer, but although this can be an economical way of feeding such snakes, chicks should not be used as an exclusive diet because they do not contain sufficient calcium for a growing snake: at most, they should be used to provide about 50% of the snake's food, the remainder being rodents or adult birds, etc.

METHODS OF FEEDING

With the exception of worms, etc., all food given to snakes should be dead. Apart from the moral aspect of feeding one live animal to another, uneaten rats and mice can badly mutilate or even kill a snake if left in its cage. A further advantage of feeding dead prey is that suitable food can be bought in bulk and frozen until required. Needless to say, the carcass must be thoroughly thawed before being offered to the snake – failure to do this is likely to cause digestive problems. Generally speaking, a healthy snake will take its food within minutes of it being placed in the cage. Occasionally, however, individuals are reluctant to feed and a number of tricks can be tried in order to stimulate their appetites. Firstly, make sure that the snake is not refusing to feed for one of the following reasons; temperature too low; shedding imminent; disease; wrong food offered; egg-laying or birth imminent (females only!). If none of these applies, try placing the food in the snake's hide-box; some species are used to finding and eating their prey in underground nests or burrows and do not like to feed in the open. For similar reasons, food may be placed in the cage in the evening and left overnight when the lights are off. Some individuals prefer their food to be a little bit 'high' – try leaving it in a warm place for twenty-four hours before offering it to the snake. Other snakes seem unable to recognise food unless it is moving – try jiggling the food in front of the snake or dragging it slowly in front of its nose a few times; this will often be enough to stimulate it to strike and begin the swallowing process. Certain species, including several of the montane kingsnakes, though normally prepared to take rodents, actually prefer other prey, for example lizards or frogs. If this is the case, a mouse anointed with the smell of the favourite food may do the trick, and in time it will probably be possible to dispense with this altogether. In this way, a dead frog or lizard may be kept frozen and used many times over by donating its smell to other, more easily obtained, food.

If all else fails, it may be necessary to force-feed the snake. This involves holding it gently behind the head with the forefinger and thumb, making sure that the rest of the body is supported, for instance, on a table. The mouth must then be opened, either with a spare finger or by an assistant using a smooth implement such as a spatula or the handle of a

47

spoon. Having done this, place the food object, which should not be too large, in the snake's mouth, head first. The snake will often clamp its jaws on to this and if gently replaced into its cage will begin to swallow of its own accord. If it does so, follow up with more food items placed near it, as once its appetite is stimulated it may well be prepared to continue feeding voluntarily.

Should this method of force-feeding be unsuccessful, more drastic measures will be necessary. Proceed as before, but when the food is in the snake's mouth, gently push it down its throat, using a smooth metal or glass rod. It may be helpful to lubricate the food slightly by dipping it into water or egg-yolk, although this is not always necessary. In order to avoid damage or stress, it is advisable to cut the food into small portions which will enter the snake's throat with the minimum of stretching, even though this may mean repeating the operation several times in order to provide a satisfactory meal. Before replacing the snake in its cage, gently massage the food down its throat by running a finger from its chin to about one-third of the way down its body (which is roughly where its stomach will be). After force-feeding, snakes should be returned gently to their cage and not disturbed for at least twelve hours, otherwise they may regurgitate their meal. Snakes which are too weak even to swallow and digest food may be kept alive by force-feeding them a liquid diet of egg-yolk fortified with liquidised mouse and/or vitamin preparations. This cocktail is most conveniently administered via a large plastic syringe with a length of rubber tubing attached to the nozzle. The tube must be passed down the throat and the fluid slowly forced out of the syringe.

Finally, a word about the 'pinkie-pump'. This is a syringe-like instrument designed to force-feed small snakes with a minimum of trauma. Several dead pink mice are placed in the barrel and forced through a tapering nozzle which is placed in the snake's mouth. A device at the bottom of the barrel ensures that the mice are liquidised before entering the nozzle. Pinkie-pumps are occasionally available, usually through society newsletters and so on, but are not at present manufactured on a commercial scale. There is a danger, because the operation is so simple, that snakes may be overfed and, invaluable though this idea can be, it should be used with caution.

CHAPTER 6

Breeding

Throughout this book, heavy emphasis is placed on breeding captive snakes. There are many reasons why this should be so: a good supply of captive-bred animals relieves pressure on wild populations; techniques which have been found to be successful with common species may be applied to some of those that are endangered; and captive-bred animals, free from disease and without the stress of capture, are more likely than wild ones to adapt successfully to captive conditions. Valid though these arguments are, however, the best reason for trying to breed snakes in captivity, in my opinion, is that only by successfully inducing them to breed can we be sure that the conditions under which we are keeping them are as near perfect as possible.

Snakes are very tough creatures and will survive under conditions which are far from ideal. This often works to their disadvantage in captivity since the fact that they remain alive is frequently construed as an indication that their requirements are being met. Many captive snakes, indeed, are merely 'survivors', lingering on only because of their ability to tolerate adverse conditions. On the other hand, those individuals which actively follow the instinct of all living things to reproduce, are behaving naturally and indicate, as far as is possible, that we have understood and provided the correct conditions.

A large number of species of snakes have now been bred in captivity, and of these, two groups may be recognised. Firstly, there are the so-called 'formula' breeders, those which invariably do breed provided that a fairly straightforward regime is adhered to. Secondly, there are those species which, although they will breed from time to time, do not seem to conform to any special pattern and may often breed when we least expect it. The difference between the two groups is basically one of understanding the environmental triggers which initiate the urge to breed, either in the males, or in the females, or both. The remainder of this chapter is devoted to explaining the techniques which have been

49

found essential, or at least beneficial, in order to breed snakes. They are necessarily based on experience with the species which are most easily bred, but many of the details will also apply to those species which breed only rarely. It is important that beginners spend some time working with the easier species because these will be more likely to produce the kind of results that will encourage perseverance with those that are less accommodating. In addition, methods which work with these easier species will probably apply, if modified slightly, to most others.

SEX DETERMINATION

It is obvious that the first step towards breeding snakes is to obtain a male and a female. Animals bought from a reliable breeder will be correctly sexed, and it may be possible to specify unrelated young. Although it may be advantageous to keep a breeding group consisting of one male and several females, it is unreasonable to expect a breeder to supply animals in this sex ratio, although surplus females may occasionally be available.

If animals are not obtained in this way, it will be necessary to determine the sexes. Very few species of snakes show sexual dimorphism, both sexes being superficially similar, but in many species, adult males can be recognised by their proportionately longer tails, associated with a greater number of scales beneath the tail (subcaudals), most easily counted on a shed skin, and a slight swelling immediately behind the cloaca, caused by the presence of the paired copulatory organs, the hemipenes. These normally lie in an inverted (inside-out) position and are only everted during mating (Plate 8). A more reliable means of detecting their presence or otherwise is to use a probe, consisting of a smooth metal, glass or plastic rod which is inserted into the cloaca and *gently* eased into one of the cavities at the base of the tail (*see* Fig. 14). In order to facilitate this operation it is advisable to lubricate the probe, with petroleum jelly, for instance, and to hold the tail straight, which may require the aid of an assistant if the snake is especially powerful. In females, it will be possible to pass the probe back only as far as the musk glands, which lie beneath the first one or two subcaudal scales, but in males it should be possible to enter one or other of the inverted hemipenes which extend to at least the ninth subcaudal scale. Extreme care must be taken in inserting the probe because damage can easily result from rough handling. It is often helpful to twirl the probe slightly between the thumb and first finger as it is inserted. Should the probe meet any resistance it should be withdrawn and inserted again, possibly on the other side of the snake.

For most adults, medium-sized snakes a probe with a diameter of 2–3 mm will be most useful, but hatchling snakes will require a smaller

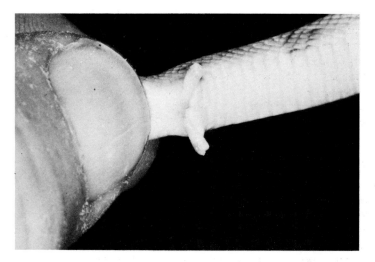

8. The everted hemipenes of a young snake (*Elaphe subocularis*). The snake has been encouraged to evert them by applying gentle pressure at the base of the tail with the thumb, which is slowly rolled upwards. (This technique is not described in the text because it requires considerable practice to perfect, and probing is more reliable.)

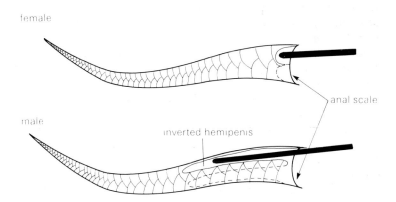

Fig. 14. Snakes can be reliably sexed by gently inserting an appropriately sized probe into the cloaca and gently moving it back to see if it will enter the inverted hemipenes.

probe, of about 1 mm diameter. Although it is possible to purchase commercially made probes, these tend to be an expensive luxury; one (of many) alternative methods is to select a number of steel knitting needles of the appropriate diameters and have them cut down, rounded off and polished.

CONDITIONING

Snakes will rarely breed unless they have been well fed on suitable food. In addition, they should be free of parasites or wounds, either of which may cause problems under the additional stress of reproduction, especially in the case of females. Furthermore, the environmental conditions have to be manipulated in such a way as to trigger the breeding instinct. No matter how healthy they are, snakes rely on outside influences such as temperature and light to 'tell them' when to develop eggs or sperm, or to go in search of a mate.

As a general rule, species which originate in temperate regions tend to be easier to breed than those from the tropics. This is because the cues which initiate breeding are more readily definable, i.e. rising temperatures and increasing day-length. Tropical species as a whole may breed as a result of more subtle factors such as changes in humidity, in the amount of rainfall or the slight drop in temperature associated with rainfall – in many cases, we just don't know.

The most useful information, therefore, that can be given applies to the temperate or subtropical species. In the wild, these species invariably mate in the spring and lay their eggs in early summer so that the young have the best possible chance of securing a reasonable amount of food before they are rendered inactive by cool weather. Alternatively, the females may retain the developing embryos in their bodies and give birth to fully developed young. In addition, spermatogenesis, the process during which the male sex cells are formed, will often only occur at temperatures which are lower than the normal preferred body temperature of the snake, i.e. during hibernation. Adult animals from which it is intended to breed should therefore be allowed to cool off during the winter, and then gradually warmed up and given the increased day-lengths which occur during the spring. In this way, the reproductive cycles of the males and the females will coincide.

There are many ways of doing this, and because the degree to which reproduction is controlled by temperature and light varies from species to species according to their origins, it is necessary to generalise. Where possible, more precise instructions are given in the species accounts. Snakes which come from areas well outside the tropics, e.g. northern Europe or northern North America, normally undergo a period of complete hibernation. This may last for six months or more, during which time temperatures may drop to near freezing point. In captivity, these species require a hibernation period of at least three months at a temperature of 4–10°C (39–50°F). Species from subtropical regions, i.e. southern North America, the Mediterranean region or southern Africa require a 'cooling-off' period of about two to two and a half months at a temperature of 10–13°C (50–55°F) and tropical species should also be cooled, but only to about 18°C (65°F). It should be noted that many tropical species, e.g. Indian pythons, as well as some subtropical ones such as indigo snakes, mate at the coolest time of the year.

Difficulties sometimes arise when the precise habitat of a species is not known, and it is important to differentiate between lowland and montane species. For instance, several of the kingsnakes and milk snakes, genus *Lampropeltis*, though occurring in Arizona, New Mexico, California and Mexico, are restricted to high mountain ranges. These species are therefore subject to long periods of very low temperatures and need to hibernate, whereas lowland species, some of them living only a few miles away, experience very little by way of seasonal temperature fluctuation. For this reason it is important to research thoroughly the natural history of the animal, especially if it is of a species which has only rarely been bred, before deciding upon a regime.

It is an advantage, if possible, to time the cooling-off period for all these snakes to coincide with the natural 'winter' of their range, but in the case of southern species maintained in the northern hemisphere, and vice versa, this is not always practicable. Adult snakes which have been taken from the wild and moved across the equator are often difficult to breed because there is a conflict between their inbuilt natural rhythm and the 'new' environmental parameters to which they are subjected. As expected, once these species are acclimatised, they often breed readily, and their offspring present none of these difficulties.

During the hibernation period, food should be withheld but water must be present at all times. In the case of small species it may be necessary to spray them lightly every week in order to prevent dehydration, although this will usually be necessary only in dry regions or if air conditioning has dehumidified the room. Reduction of temperature should be carried out slowly over at least two weeks in order to avoid shock to the animals, and it is important that they are not fed during the two weeks immediately prior to cooling, otherwise undigested food may remain in their stomachs, with disastrous results. Any sick or underweight animals should not be hibernated – they would be unlikely to breed successfully anyway.

In nature, the decrease in temperature during autumn is also accompanied by shorter day-lengths. In most species which have been studied, it appears that day-length is of less importance to snakes than temperature. This would seem logical considering that most of the species which are commonly kept are secretive and fairly oblivious to day-length. However, certain species *have* responded to the experimental increase of day-lengths and, since this is not difficult to arrange, it may be worth doing. Keepers in Europe, North America, South Africa and Australasia (i.e. the majority) who house their animals in rooms with windows will need to do little by way of light manipulation; the animals will key in to the existing light regime, especially if it coincides with temperature fluctuations. Otherwise it will be necessary to install artificial lighting, preferably with a time-switch, to keep control (*see also* Chapter 3).

Young snakes from which it is hoped to breed need not be hibernated or cooled off during their first winter. If they are maintained at normal temperatures they will usually continue feeding and therefore reach sexual maturity at an earlier age. It appears that hibernation is only necessary during the year in which the snakes are to breed, although animals which have been kept under constant or incorrect regimes for a long time may take up to two years to begin their cycles.

Finally, there is some confusion over the importance of Vitamin D3 to snakes. Although it has been shown that many species of lizards will not breed (or even survive) without this, it is still uncertain what part, if any, it plays in snakes. One would expect it to be more important to basking species such as some of the whipsnakes than to secretive ones, but good results have occasionally been obtained after using supplements of this vitamin. Current opinion seems to favour its use, not as a matter of course, but in the case of snakes which have failed to breed even though conditions are correct in all other respects. Vitamin D3 is necessary in the system to facilitate the uptake of calcium. Calcium is essential for the formation of skeletal material, but also for the maintenance of muscle tone. Therefore, snakes which lack calcium or Vitamin D3 become flaccid and listless (they rarely become so deficient that the skeleton is affected) and so the 'feel' of a snake is important in assessing whether or not supplements are necessary. If need be, a supplement containing Vitamin D3 and calcium, available from reptile dealers, may be sprinkled over the food.

PAIRING

Conditioned males and females from which it is hoped to breed may be paired in several ways. Some keepers favour keeeping the sexes separate until they are ready to mate. The snakes are then put together at a time which is considered to be optimum for mating to take place. Snakes which have an urge to mate often become restless and crawl around their cage during the day, and may refuse food. A more precise means of estimating the state of their reproductive cycle is to palpate the females in order to detect the presence of ovarian follicles, i.e. the potential eggs. To do this it is necessary to hold the snake lightly and allow it to crawl through the hand while pressing gently on the ventral surface with a finger. If follicles are present they will be felt as small hard lumps, fairly evenly spaced from about half-way along the snake almost to its cloaca. At this point the snake will be receptive to mating and if a conditioned male is available the female should be placed in his cage.

Courtship often takes place almost immediately, followed by mating. During courtship the male will often glide around the cage following the female, eventually sliding his body forward on top of hers until their cloacae are adjacent. They may make frequent twitching motions and in some species the male may bite the back of the female's neck. Copulation may last anything from a few minutes to several hours, and the snakes should be disturbed as little as possible during this time. It is advisable to allow the pair to mate several times to ensure fertilisation, and this will usually occur over a period of two to three weeks, after which time the female will cease to be receptive and ignore the attentions of the male. If a male seems reluctant to mate at any time, activity can often be stimulated by the addition of another male to the group, or by placing the pair together immediately after the female has shed her skin.

An alternative method is to leave the pair together all of the time, relying on the snakes themselves to decide when they are most receptive. The only real disadvantages of this method are that mating often goes unobserved and so accurate records cannot be kept, and that one male can only be mated with a fairly limited number of females. In all other respects the system is perfectly acceptable.

It may sometimes be useful to know definitely whether a fertile mating has taken place and this can be achieved by squeezing a small drop of fluid from the female's cloaca and looking for the presence of spermatozoa under a low-powered microscope. Spermatozoa are elongated tadpole-like organisms and, if healthy, should be moving. The presence of no spermatozoa, or of inactive ones, is an indication that the male is sterile (assuming that mating has taken place), often caused by a failure to cool him down sufficiently during the previous winter (which is when spermatogenesis occurs). There is little reliable information on the number of females which a male can successfully fertilise during a single breeding season, but the records of Bob Applegate of El Cajon, California seem to indicate that fertility diminishes after about eight matings. However, after a brief respite, the male is again capable of producing viable spermatozoa, but only in the case of species in which cooling is not essential (in this instance *Lampropeltis getulus*).

EGG-LAYING/BIRTH

Females of live-bearing species, e.g. the boas, garter snakes, etc. will normally seek out the warmer parts of their cage during pregnancy, and there is little by way of special maintenance required. As birth becomes imminent, small species may appreicate an area of moist sphagnum in which to deposit their young.

For those species which lay eggs, it will be necessary to enable the female to find a suitable place in which to deposit them. Unfortunately, it is rarely possible to forecast the exact time of egg-laying since the period between mating and laying is subject to a great deal of variation; this is partly due to its dependence on temperature but, more importantly, to the capability of many, if not all, species to store sperm for several weeks or even months before the eggs themselves are fertilised. Gravid snakes become swollen with eggs some weeks before egg-laying is due, but the swelling moves down towards the cloaca during the later stages. In addition, a useful pointer to the date of laying is the phenomenon known as the pre-laying slough. It seems that female snakes invariably slough their skins five to twelve days before laying. Although the exact period varies between species, it is more or less constant within species, and once this is established it is a simple matter to predict laying.

It has been found that, under captive conditions, many species of snakes will lay more than one clutch of eggs during each breeding season. If it is intended to exploit this ability, the females must be in prime condition before the breeding season, and feeding should continue throughout the period before egg-laying. The animals are then mated as soon as possible after laying (second clutches are sometimes produced without a further mating but fertility is usually low) and if the animals have become active early in the year, it may even be possible to obtain a third clutch. From various records it appears that the period of time between mating and egg-laying is shorter for second and third clutches than it is for the first clutch. There is also a trend towards smaller clutches and a slightly higher incidence of infertility in these clutches. However, provided that the animals are in good health, there is no evidence to suggest that multiple clutching has any adverse effect on females.

All snake eggs are contained in a semi-permeable, flexible shell, and absorb water throughout their development. In nature, therefore, females seek out a damp substrate in which to lay, and this may consist of a pile of decomposing vegetation, rotting wood or the like. In captivity, suitable substrates include chopped sphagnum moss, peat or vermiculite, all of which are reasonably sterile materials, Whichever is used, it should be moistened slightly; this is best achieved by saturating it in water and then squeezing out all the surplus until there is no free water left. It is then placed in a container such as a plastic box of the appropriate size (the female should be able to coil up completely in the container) and placed in the cage. Some breeders like to give the female a bit of seclusion by cutting a small hole in the lid and allowing her to enter through this, rather than leaving the box open. If the drawer-type cage is employed, the egg-laying container should be placed in the drawer, and if plastic bowls are used in lieu of a drawer, one of these can act as the egg-laying container.

The female will begin to spend most of her time in the container during the few days immediately prior to laying, and an inspection should be made for eggs at least once a day. As soon as eggs are found, they should be removed for artificial incubation, the only exceptions to this rule being a handful of python species in which the female broods her eggs by coiling around them, in which case a somewhat different arrangement will be necessary (see Chapter 7).

INCUBATION

The incubation of snake eggs is not a difficult operation provided that a few simple rules are followed. Vermiculite of a fairly fine grade is the preferred medium. This should be moist but not waterlogged; equal parts by weight of vermiculite and water give the right consistency, but complete accuracy is not essential once some experience has been gained. The eggs may be kept in the container in which they were laid if vermiculite has been used, but it is generally preferable to remove them to a clean plastic box. If they have stuck together into a cluster it is best not to attempt to separate them, otherwise damage can easily be done, but if they are freshly laid they will usually come apart with little trouble, and this can have advantages. The eggs are placed in depressions in the vermiculite in such a way that each is in contact with the substrate but not completely covered (this is where difficulties sometimes arise with large clumps of eggs), and the lid of the box replaced. It does not seem too important whether or not there are small airholes in the lid, although if the container is totally airtight it may be necessary to open it briefly every week or so. (It is important, of course, that air is available for the baby snakes once they hatch.) During incubation the eggs will absorb water and swell. Initially they will retain a fairly uniform shape, usually slightly cylindrical, and be white or cream in colour. However, as the developing embryo absorbs the yolk, the shell will become misshapen and may also become discoloured. This is perfectly normal, but should the egg begin to develop patches of mould early on in development, the chances are that it is infertile. Infertile eggs are also often smaller than the rest of the clutch and may be yellowish. If they are not firmly attached to the rest of the clutch, infertile or bad eggs should be removed in order to prevent the mould spreading to other, good, eggs. However, in my experience, good eggs invariably hatch, even if they have mould on their surface.

Temperatures at which eggs should be incubated are subject to some variation, but a temperature of about 28°C (82°F) is suitable for most temperate and subtropical species, while those of tropical species require slightly warmer conditions, about 30°C (86°F). It is not necessary to maintain these temperatures precisely, but if fluctuations can be kept to a minimum, the incubation period can be predicted more accurately. In order to do this it may be necessary to construct a special cabinet in which the eggs are kept. This need not be elaborate, but should contain a reliable thermostat, connected to a heating element, such as a length of heat tape or heating cable coiled underneath a false floor. Shelves onto which the boxes containing eggs are placed should stop a few inches short of the back and front of the cabinet so that heat rising from the heat source can circulate without restriction (*see* Fig. 15). A slightly more sophisticated means of ensuring this is to install a small fan which blows a current of air across the heater.

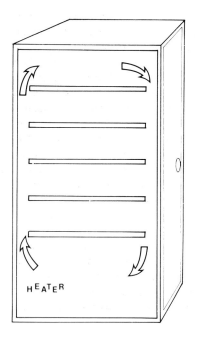

Fig. 15. A home-built incubator for snake-eggs, viewed from the side. The shelves stop short of the front and back, allowing warm air from the heater (which is normally electrically operated) to circulate. A more sophisticated design would incorporate a small fan to ensure an even temperature throughout the cabinet, but this is not usually necessary. The eggs are placed in small plastic boxes half-filled with damp vermiculite, and labelled with the species name and date of laying.

Incubation periods vary between species, but are often within the range of 60–90 days at 28°C (82°F). When the young snake is fully formed, the shell of the egg will have begun to shrink around its coiled shape. Shortly after this the young snake will slit the egg-shell, using a small 'egg-tooth' on its snout. Very often, it will make several slits and may remain in its shell for up to two days before venturing out. It should be allowed to come out in its own time, although if an egg is known to be overdue, for instance if its clutch-mates have already hatched, then it may be worth cutting into the shell in an attempt to help it. This rarely works, however, and it will usually be found that the young snake is either dead, deformed or very weak. (Nevertheless, I have heard of two separate cases, both involving gopher snakes, *Pituophis melanoleucus*, where it proved necessary to slit the shells with a blade in order to improve the hatch-rate). Once the whole clutch has hatched, the hatchlings should be removed to rearing cages. As they will not feed until they have sloughed their skins, usually within one week of hatching, they may be housed together even if they are of cannibalistic species, but rearing is best carried out individually.

REARING THE YOUNG

Hatchling snakes are best housed in small plastic containers (lunch-boxes or shoe-boxes, according to which side of the Atlantic you live). Each box should contain a small amount of substrate, a water bowl, a piece of crumpled or folded paper or card (as a retreat) and one snake. These boxes are most easily accommodated on a shelf fitted with a heat tape as described in Chapter 2, and if large numbers of young are to be reared it is worth making a special rack for them, with the shelves arranged in such a way that a standard-sized box just fits – this will eliminate the need to tape or clip the lids onto the boxes (*see* palte 2). Each young snake should be given an identification number and a small record card attached to the top of its box. As soon as it has completed its initial slough, it should be offered food. If some of the young are to be sold or otherwise disposed of, it will be necessary to sex them, using the probing technique described above.

Once the young snakes are feeding regularly they will begin to grow quite rapidly and it may be necessary to move them on to an intermediate-sized cage before finally accommodating them in permanent quarters. Many young snakes, notably king snakes and ratsnakes, can reach sexual maturity in just under two years and will produce eggs during their second summer. Larger species, such as the pythons and boas, may take considerably longer.

BREEDING SYSTEMS

As more and more snakes are being bred in captivity, the problem of inbreeding will begin to loom ever larger. This is especially true of some of the stocks of colour-mutants (*see* page 61) where large numbers of animals are produced from a single common ancestor, or in the case of some of the rarer or protected species of which only a handful of individuals comprised the original breeding stock.

The problem may briefly be described as follows. Every animal within a population will carry a number of 'lethal' genes. These are genes which are in some way abnormal and, if expressed, would cause the animal to die (or prevent its development). However, since each individual has a 'double dose' of each gene, the chances are that at least one of each pair is normal, and this will be sufficient for the animal to operate (in other words, the normal gene is dominant to the lethal gene), but if both genes are abonormal, the lethal gene will be expressed. Now, if closely related animals are continually interbred, the chances of both the male and the female containing the same lethal gene become progressively higher mathematically, and so more and more offspring possess a double dose of the lethal gene. This applies to every lethal gene which may have been present in the first place and also to the many other genes which, though not lethal, may programme for reduced fitness. The outcome is an increased frequency of lethal and sublethal genes which together seriously weaken the stock; this is known as 'inbreeding depression' and usually becomes noticeable after about five generations of brother-sister matings.

The only sure way of avoiding inbreeding depression is to bring fresh genes (i.e. fresh blood) into the colony each generation so that any lethal and sublethal genes which are present are continually diluted, just as they are in nature. Fresh blood may consist of wild-caught animals if they are legally available, or captive-bred animals from *unrelated* stock. This is where problems are often encountered, either because the present stock has some unique characteristic which it is wished to retain, e.g. a colour variety, or because wild stocks are no longer available. In these cases it is vitally important to keep an accurate record of the pedigree of each snake in the colony. Similarly, if any stock are bought or sold, the predigree must accompany them so that in generations to come it will be possible to ascertain which animals are related to which.

In planning a breeding system for animals to which the above remarks are likely to apply, one way of decreasing the incidence of inbreeding depression is to use a maximum avoidance system. This is a method of ensuring that the gene pool is kept as large as possible and that lethal genes are prevented from accumulating any faster than is necessary. A minimum of eight pairs are required if the system is to be kept simple, and these are numbered 1–8. In the next generation, the new pairs (n.p.) are made up from the offspring of the old pairs (o.p.) as follows:

n.p.1 consists of a male from o.p.1 + female from o.p.2

n.p.2 consists of a male from o.p.3 + female from o.p.4

n.p.3 consists of a male from o.p.5 + female from o.p.6

n.p.4 consists of a male from o.p.7 + female from o.p.8

n.p.5 consists of a male from o.p.2 + female from o.p.1

n.p.6 consists of a male from o.p.4 + female from o.p.3

n.p.7 consists of a male from o.p.6 + female from o.p.5

n.p.8 consists of a male from o.p.8 + female from o.p.7

If this is done for each generation the rate of inbreeding will be just over 1.5% each time and the colony could survive for many years without the addition of fresh blood. As a practical arrangement, it would probably be necessary to incorporate pairs from more than one collection into the scheme, with an agreement to exchange several young at each generation.

SELECTIVE BREEDING

I approach this aspect of snake-keeping with a great deal of trepidation. Over the years a number of mutant snakes have cropped up, either caught in the wild or bred in captivity, and it is only natural, given the novelty value of these animals, that breeders will want to exercise their talents by breeding from them in an attempt to create new strains. Whereas some of these animals are very pretty, others are aesthetically dwarfed by their naturally occurring counterparts. However, all of them have their following and they must obviously be considered.

Many of the colour mutants are controlled by fairly straightforward mendelian inheritance. In other words, if two mutants are crossed, all of the resultant offspring will also be mutants, but if a mutant is crossed with a normal animal, the offspring will look normal but carry the mutant gene as a recessive. If these are subsequently interbred, one-quarter of the offspring (statistically speaking) will be normal, one-quarter will be mutant and the other half will look normal but be carriers (heterozygotes) like their parents. Characteristics which are controlled in this way are amelanism (the absence of black pigment) and albinism (the absence of all pigments except haemoglobin). In several species, notably corn snakes, *Elaphe guttata*, a number of different colour mutants have arisen and these can be combined to give a wide range of different strains.

Problems which accompany the propagation of mutants are of two types. Firstly, the selection of breeding stock from a small number of original, naturally occurring, mutants can rapidly lead to inbreeding depression, as described above. In fact, it is relatively easy to prevent this by crossing out to normal animals every few generations, but regaining the mutation can then take several years and breeders are naturally reluctant to do this. The other problem concerns the heterozygous animals which are produced as a by-product of this selective breeding; it is not possible to determine their genetic make-up from appearances and the danger of these animals being sold as normals, either intentionally or accidentally, are very real.

Rather more serious is the production of hybrid snakes. This may occur either in response to the lack of a mate belonging to the correct subspecies, i.e. in the case of rare subspecies, or due to the breeder's penchant for experimentation. Indeed, several enterprising breeders have produced hybrids from parents belonging to different species or even different genera, e.g. *Pituophis melanoleucus* × *Elaphe guttata*! The very fact that this can be achieved is enormously interesting from a scientific point of view, but the prospect of such unnatural progeny getting into general circulation does not auger well for the future of our hobby – few people would wish to see snake-breeding go down the same road as that taken by the dog or fancy goldfish fraternity, with their obsession for grotesque and pathetic forms. We therefore rely entirely on the honesty of breeders to maintain genetic integrity of the snakes which they offer for sale.

CHAPTER 7

Family Boidae – Boas and Pythons

As well as including all five of the world's giant snakes, the Boidae also contains a large number of smaller but no less interesting species. Many of these are regularly kept and bred both by beginners and experts, and provide ample scope for a varied collection. A few species, such as the common boa, *Boa constrictor*, stand out as firm favourites, but in recent years other species have become almost as popular.

Since the species comprising this family are greatly diversified, it is not possible to generalise about their maintenance, but a few comments can be made. Most boas and pythons are tropical snakes and require consistently high temperatures, about 25–30°C (77–88°F), if they are to thrive. However, the secret of breeding success appears to be a slight reduction in temperature, to about 18–20°C (64–68°F) for a few months of the year, possibly accompanied by an increase in humidity. Many species mate during this cool period, but others may be stimulated by the increasing temperatures following a cooling-off period, in much the same way as many subtropical colubrids.

A basic difference between the pythons and boas concerns their reproductive habits: whereas the boas give birth to living young, the pythons lay eggs. Breeding has now been achieved for most of the species which are commonly kept, although there are a few which have defied all attempts to induce them to breed regularly. This fact, together with their undoubted commercial appeal, provides a challenge to the would-be breeder which is probably unequalled by any other group of snakes.

In order to simplify the information, the boas will be dealt with first, followed by the pythons.

Subfamilies Boinae, Calabarinae and Ericinae – Boas

A number of subfamilies of the Boidae go under the popular name of 'boas', including the three subfamilies above, which provide various species frequently kept in captivity. A number of species belonging to the boinae (true boas) possess heat-sensitive pits in their upper and lower jaws, but, unlike those of the pythons, these are situated *between* the scales.

Acrantophis dumerili   Dumeril's Ground Boa (Colour Plate 1)

Size: to 200 cm (80 in)
Range: Madagascar

Dumeril's ground boa is a heavy-bodied species with a narrow, pointed head. Its intricate markings consist of a network of irregular dark brown blotches over a tan or pale brown ground. These markings tend to be heavier on the flanks of the snake, being reduced to a narrow bar across the back, where the marking on one flank meets that on the other. The head is pale grey marked with a number of dark lines, including one running through the eye.

Housing and feeding of this species is similar to that of the following one. Temperature about 30°C (86°F) during summer, but night-time temperatures allowed to fall to 25°C (77F) during the winter, autumn and spring in order to induce breeding. Adults mature at approximately four years of age.

Availability: This species is totally protected. However, small numbers of breeding animals are maintained in South Africa, Europe and the United States, and these produce a few surplus young each year. Prices are high, due to the rarity of the species and its low reproductive potential.

Breeding data (from literature and M. Hammock)

Time of mating: November–January
Gestation period: 200–300 days (average 240 days)
Litter size: 6–9 (average of 4 litters, 7.8)
Size of neonates: 41–45 cm (16–18 in)
First food: Mice, small birds

Acrantophis madagascariensis   Madagascan Ground Boa

Size: to about 300 cm (120 in)
Range: Northern Madagascar

This species is very similar superficially to the common boa of South America. A jet black line joins the eye to the angle of the mouth and the back is brown with an indistinct zigzag pattern of light and dark. The upper flanks are paler brown, marked with oval black blotches and smaller black spots while the lower flanks have a series of large pale-centred brown blotches. The whole surface of head and body is highly iridescent.

The species requires a large cage and a temperature of 25–30°C (77–86°F). A hide-box and a large water bowl in which the snake can soak are essential. Diet consists of rodents, although some specimens prefer birds, e.g. chicks, pigeons and quail. Breeding appears to be stimulated by a slight drop in temperature, to about 20°C (68°F) during the winter. Several years are taken for the animals to reach sexual maturity, which is attained at about 190 cm (75 in).

Availability: *See* previous species.

Breeding data (from literature)

Time of mating:	December–January (northern hemisphere) May, August (southern hemisphere)
Gestation period:	223–285 days (average 250 days)
Litter size:	2–6 (average of 4 litters, 3.75)
Size of neonates:	57–71 cm (22–28 in)
First food:	Adult mice

KEY REFERENCE:

Branch, W. R. and Erasmus, H. (1976). 'Reproduction in Madagascar ground and tree boas'. *Int. Zoo Yb*. Vol. 16: 78–80.

Boa constrictor Common Boa (Plate 9 and Colour Plate 2)

Size: to 300 cm (120 in), occasionally more
Range: from northern Mexico, through Central America and well into South America, taking in several of the West Indian islands

The common boa needs little description. Basically a grey, brown or pinkish snake with a series of dark saddles running down the back. These become darker and more closely spaced towards the tail and in some forms tend towards red. The head is gracefully wedge-shaped, with a dark line which starts at the eye and then becomes gradually wider as it passes backward to the angle of the jaw. Eight subspecies are recognised by most authorities, all of which are kept in captivity, although to a varying degree. Their identification can be difficult if their natural origin is not known, because there is much individual variation within each population and, furthermore, it is probable that many of the captive-bred

9. Common Boa, *Boa constrictor*, very popular, especially among beginners.

hatchlings which come onto the market may be hybrids between closely related forms. The Argentinian subspecies *B. c. occidentalis*, however, deserves special mention since it is so unlike any of the other forms. Instead of saddles, the dark markings are greatly extended to form a network over the whole of the snake, which is otherwise silver-grey.

Care of the common boa is normally straightforward, although new-born snakes can be delicate, being especially susceptible, in my experience, to cold. Adults and young require a temperature approaching 30°C (86°F), although this may be allowed to drop slightly at night. Diet is mice, rats and rabbits, according to the size of the snake, and some individuals will, if necessary, take chicks and other birds. Feeding is not normally a problem unless conditions are incorrect. This species likes to climb and its cage should be high enough to include a substantial branch. In addition, if an overhead heat source is used to boost the general background heating during the day (a good arrangement), it is beneficial to construct a strong shelf below this so that the snake can bask. A large water bowl is essential as this species frequently likes to submerge itself completely, especially when about to shed its skin. Some individuals make use of a hide-box, but others will ignore this and spend their time resting in an exposed position.

Animals from which it is hoped to breed should be cooled down to about 22°C (72°F) – 20°C (68°F) minimum – for about two months in the winter, and mating will usually take place at this time. However, common boas are unreliable breeders and few keepers can claim consistent results.

Not only do healthy snakes fail to breed when conditions are seemingly perfect, but others do breed when least expected. It is therefore difficult to give hard and fast advice because methods which work with one pair of snakes do not always work with another; but the key to success would appear to be the temperature drop, as mentioned above, possibly a slight increase in humidity, and the possession of a compatible pair.

Availability: Despite legal protection over most of its range, the common boa is one of the most freely available species in its family. Baby boas enter the pet trade frequently, although they vary in quality and price, and captive-bred youngsters are also listed occasionally – these are always in great demand.

Breeding data (from literature, H. Cohen)

Time of mating:	Recorded for almost every month of the year but mostly during winter
Gestation period:	127–249 days (average 167 days)
Litter size:	8–49 (average of 37 clutches, 24.8)
Mortality:	Very few stillbirths reported
Size of neonates:	35–60 cm (14–24 in)
First food:	Half to three-quarter grown mice

KEY REFERENCES:

Chiras, S. (1979). 'Husbandry and reproduction of the red-tail boa, *Boa constrictor ssp.*' *Proc. 3rd Ann. Symp. on Captive Propagation and Husbandry*, 95–98.

Wells, E. (1980). 'A diurnal variation's effect on a captive breeding of *Boa constrictor constrictor*'. *Proc. 4th Ann. Symp. on Captive Propagation and Husbandry*, 11–16.

Candoia aspera Pacific Ground Boa

Size: to about 75 cm (30 in)
Range: Pacific islands, including New Guinea

This species has a short, stout body covered with heavily keeled scales. In coloration it is dark reddish-brown with obscure black-edged brown blotches along the back. The amount of red on the body is variable, and is more prominent on the undersurface.

This interesting small boa requires only a small cage. The substrate may be of bark chippings or dead leaves, and a hide-box and water bowl are essential. In its native habitat it occupies forest floors in areas of high humidity, such as along river banks, and in captivity it seems to be necessary to spray its cage frequently in order to avoid problems with skin shedding and in order to induce it to eat. Although most specimens will eat small mice, some will only take lizards, which may be its natural prey. There are no records of captive breeding of this species, but newborn young are small and may be difficult to start feeding.

Availability: This species is totally protected. Small numbers appear on lists occasionally, the origin of which is unclear. Since there are so few of this species in collections, there is little hope of regular supplies of captive-bred young.

Candoia carinata   Pacific Boa

> Size: to about 120 cm (48 in), occasionally longer
> Range: Pacific islands, including New Hebrides and the Solomons

This species is also stout-bodied, though less so than the previous one. It is variable in colour and may be grey, cream, brown or brick-red with a darker undulating line along the back (giving it the alternative common name of 'viper boa').

It requires a medium-sized cage with a dry substrate, a hide-box and a water bowl. It climbs occasionally and provision should be made for this by including a stout branch. A temperature of 25–30°C (77–86°F) is required, although this must be lowered to about 20°C (68°F) for at least two months if it is hoped to breed from the animals. Diet is mice, and this species normally feeds more readily than the previous one.

Availability: This species, though totally protected, is bred in fairly large numbers by several specialist snake-breeders. Since demand for it is not especially high, there should be little trouble in obtaining young, although, as with all members of the family, legal requirements may make the transfer of even captive-bred specimens from one country to another tedious.

Breeding data (from literature)

Time of mating:	April–May
Gestation period:	165–195 days
Litter size:	5–64
Mortality rate:	Of 7 reported litters, over 50% of all young were born dead, including 2 complete litters consisting of 33 and 64 young
Size of neonates:	22–24 cm ($8\frac{1}{2}$–$9\frac{1}{2}$ in) in length but extremely slender
First food:	Despite their small size, some neonates will accept pink mice – others will only accept lizards such as *Anolis* spp

KEY REFERENCE:

Fauci, J. (1981). 'Breeding and rearing of captive Solomons Islands ground boas, *Candoia carinata paulseni*'. *Herp. Review* 12(2); 60–61. (This important paper was also published in the *Proceedings of the 3rd Annual Symposium on Captive Propagation and Husbandry*, 1979.)

Corallus caninus   Emerald Tree Boa (Colour Plate 3)

Size: to 150 cm (60 in)
Range: Northern South America

As its name suggests, the emerald tree boa is a bright green, arboreal snake. It closely parallels the green tree python (*see* below) in both appearance and habits, but differs from it in having the heat-sensitive facial pits between the scales of the upper lip, and in giving birth to live young. In the adults, the uniform green dorsal coloration is broken only by irregular white markings along the dorsal midline, while the ventral surface is yellow or cream. Juveniles are dimorphic, and may be bright yellow or brick-red, with white markings as in the adult.

This species is totally arboreal, rarely venturing down onto the ground, even to eat or drink. It rests in a characteristic position, with its coils draped over a horizontal bough, and may drink from water which collects in its coils. It eats rodents, bats and birds. In captivity, it requires a tall cage with a suitable branch on which to rest. A temperature of 28–35°C (82–95°F) is required, and humidity should be fairly high, at least 50%. The snakes will normally eat rodents, but some individuals apparently prefer chicks. Food is normally offered on forceps. The stimulus for inducing matings is not well established, but a slight drop in temperature, coupled with increased humidity through spraying, appears to be effective in some cases. Sexual maturity may be reached at an age of about two years.

Breeding data (from literature)

Time of mating:	December–March
Gestation period:	180–220 days
Litter size:	1–15 (average of 9 litters, 7.1)
Mortality:	Stillbirths are fairly frequent, and one case of cannibalism by the mother has been reported
Size of neonates:	40–47 cm (16–18$\frac{1}{2}$ in)
First food:	Usually lizards at first, then small mice

KEY REFERENCE:
   Murphy, J. B., Barker, D. G. and Tryon, B. W. (1978). 'Miscellaneous notes on the reproductive biology of reptiles. 2. Eleven species of the families Boidae, genera *Candoia*, *Corallus*, *Epicrates* and *Python*'. *J. Herp.* 12(3); 385–390.

Corallus enhydris   Tree Boa (including Cooke's Tree Boa)

   Size: to about 140 cm (56 in), occasionally larger
   Range: South America

This variable species is divided into several subspecies, the identity of which can be difficult unless their origin is known. Most specimens are brown or grey, generously covered with regularly shaped dark blotches, some of which have lighter centres. Others are uniformly coloured in olive, yellowish or tan.

   Like the previous species, this is a highly arboreal snake which spends much of its time resting on boughs. In captivity it tends to be rather less temperamental than *C. caninus* and usually feeds well, although it is frequently aggressive and unpleasant to handle. A temperature of 25–30°C (77–86°F) is required, and breeding behaviour is induced by lowering this by about 5°C (9°F) in the winter, mating taking place at this time.

   Availability: Apart from the common boa, this species is probably the most frequently imported of the South American snakes. Captive-bred animals are available only very infrequently.

Breeding data (from literature)

   Time of mating: December–January
   Gestation period: Around 190 days
   Litter size: 2–12 (average of 6 litters, 7.8)
   Mortality: Stillbirths recorded, but rare
   Size of neonates: 35–50 cm (14–20 in)
   First food: Lizards, e.g. *Anolis* spp, or force-fed pink mice

KEY REFERENCE:
   Stafford, P. (1981). 'Observations on the captive breeding of Cooke's tree boa (*Corallus enhydris cookii*)'. *Herptile* 6(4):15–16.

Epicrates cenchria   Rainbow Boa (Colour Plate 4)

Size: to 200 cm (80 in)
Range: South America

The rainbow boa, of which a number of subspecies are recognised, is a powerful semi-arboreal species which occurs in a variety of habitats. Its coloration varies according to subspecies, but the ground colour is usually tan, orange, reddish-brown or brown. The subspecies *E. c. cenchria*, known as the Brazilian rainbow boa (although it is also found in adjacent parts of South America), is one of the most attractive forms. A series of black rings, some of them interlocking, is arranged along the dorsal midline, on a ground colour of rich orange. Alternating with these on the flanks are smaller black rings with light centres, and the head is marked with several black stripes. The whole of the body is iridescent. The most commonly available subspecies, *E. c. maurus*, is often uniformly coloured in deep reddish-brown, the black circles being only faintly discernible, whilst *E. c. alvarezi*, from Argentina, is pale brown to orange with intricate black markings on the back and flanks.

This species, in all its forms, is one of the most adaptable of the tropical Boidae. It requires a medium-sized cage, which should be tall enough to allow for the fitting of a stout branch. A large water bowl is essential as the snake likes to submerge itself completely for long periods. Its diet consists of mice and small rats, although birds are also accepted if necessary. The temperature should be 25–30°C (77–86°F) during the summer, but if breeding is to be attempted this should be dropped to about 20°C (68°F) for at least six weeks in the winter. The animals take about three years to reach 150 cm (60 in), at which size they are sexually mature.

Availability: This is not a rare boa, and it has a wide range. Therefore, specimens are available from time to time, but the most desirable subspecies (e.g. *alvarezi* and *cenchria*) are the most expensive. Captive-bred animals are available, but are quickly taken.

Breeding data (from literature and H. Cohen)

Time of mating:	Most months of the year
Gestation period:	180–210 days
Litter size:	1–23 (average of 30 litters, 9.7)
Mortality rate:	Stillbirths are quite frequent, especially in litters born to young females
Size of neonates:	39–59 cm ($15\frac{1}{2}$–$23\frac{1}{2}$ in)
First food:	Young mice

KEY REFERENCE:

Brunner, J. C. (1977). 'Captive breeding of Colombian rainbow boas, *Epicrates cenchria crassus*'. *Proc. 2nd Ann. Symp. on Captive Propagation and Husbandry*, 39–47.

Hine, R. (1988). 'Captive breeding of the Brazilian rainbow boa, *Epicrates cenchria cenchria*'. *BHS Bulletin* (23): 25–29.

Epicrates striatus Haitian Boa

Size: to 280 cm (112 in)
Range: Hispaniola, Bahamas

E. striatus is a slender boa with a head which is distinct from the neck. The ground colour is grey, brown or reddish-brown and a series of closely arranged squarish blotches of dark brown or maroon runs along the back. A row of smaller dark blotches runs along each flank.

Cages for this species should be tall, and equipped with a well-anchored branch and a large water bowl. Adults will eat mice, small rats and birds (e.g. chicks), and a temperature of 25–30°C (77–86°F) is required. Adults should be cooled down to about 20°C (68°F) in the winter and it may also be useful to increase the relative humidity at this time by spraying.

Availability: Apart from the rainbow boa, this is the only species of *Epicrates* which is offered for sale with any degree of regularity. Most of these specimens are wild-caught.

Breeding data (from literature)

Time of mating:	April–May
Gestation period:	180 days
Litter size:	6–22 (average of 7 litters, 14)
Mortality:	Stillbirths occurred in several litters, and one consisted entirely of dead young
Size of neonates:	40–50 cm (16–20 in)
First food:	Lizards, e.g. *Anolis* spp, and pink mice, which may have to be force-fed. They are also reported to accept dead fish

Other *Epicrates* species

A number of other species of *Epicrates* species are available from time to time, including *E. angulifer*, the Cuban boa, *E. inornatus*, the Puerto Rico boa and *E. subflavus*, the Jamaican boa. Their care is similar to that given above, save that variation in size between the species will obviously control such parameters as cage-size and diet.

All these species are fully protected, but small breeding nuclei do exist, mainly in North America. They are unlikely to produce animals in sufficient numbers to make them generally available, but are important contributions to the future of these species, the habitats of which are mostly under threat. Information on the care and breeding of several species and subspecies can be obtained from the following paper:

Huff T. (1977). 'Captive propagation and husbandry of *Epicrates* at the Reptile Breeding Foundation'. *Proc. 2nd Ann Symp. on Captive Breeding and Propagation,* 103–112.

Eryx colubrinus   Kenyan Sand Boa, Egyptian Sand Boa (depending on subspecies) (Colour Plate 5)

    Size: to about 65 cm (26 in)
    Range: North and East Africa, Arabian peninsula

All the sand boas are short stout snakes with small heads, not distinct from the neck, and short tails. The present species is yellow or cream in colour, with a series of connecting large brown or orange blotches along the back. The markings of the subspecies *loveridgei*, the Kenyan sand boa, are normally brighter than those of the nominate subspecies *colubrinus*, but both are variable.

Sand boas are among the easiest of snakes to keep in captivity. They spend most of their time below the surface and should be given a good layer of sand or wood-shavings in which to burrow. If sand is used, it should be of the smooth-running type, such as horticultural silver sand. Apart from this, a small water bowl is all that is required, although if a flat rock is placed on the sand the snakes will often rest beneath this. A temperature of 25–30°C (77–86°F) is required during the day, and this can be allowed to fall to about 20°C (68°F) at night. Feeding is rarely a problem − the snakes will quickly sense the presence of a mouse on the surface of the substrate and emerge to eat it, usually within minutes. Breeding has been achieved regularly, the adults being cooled down slightly in the winter in order to stimulate mating in the spring or early summer. The young grow quickly and will breed at 2 years of age, by which time they measure about 40 cm (16 in).

Availability: Wild-caught Egyptian sand boas, *E. c. colubrinus*, are frequently available at present. *E. c. loveridgei* is protected but is being bred by a number of breeders and, hopefully, supplies of this interesting snake will improve.

Breeding data (from literature)

Time of mating: June–August
Gestation period: 120–180 days
Litter size: 4–17 (average of 7 clutches, 10.5)
Mortality: No reports of stillbirths
Size of neonates: 13.5–19 cm ($5\frac{1}{4}$–$7\frac{1}{2}$ in)
First food: Pink mice

KEY REFERENCE:
McLain, J. M. (1981). 'Reproduction in captive Kenyan sand boas, *Eryx colubrinus loveridgei*'. *Proc. 5th Ann. Symp. on Captive Propagation and Husbandry*, 76–79.

Eryx conicus Rough-scaled Sand Boa

Size: to 90 cm (28 in)
Range: Pakistan, India

This species is similar in appearance to the previous one, save that its markings are not nearly so well defined, and the scales are raised. Its captive care is also identical, but this species has not received as much attention from breeders, only two clutches being reported, of 4 and 20 young.

Several other species of sand boas are offered from time to time, including *Eryx jaculus*, the javelin sand boa, and *E. johnii*, John's sand boa. Care of all these species is much as described above, but reproductive data, which is lacking for most of them, may vary slightly.

KEY REFERENCE:
Sorenson, D. (1986). 'The genus *Eryx*'. *Proc. 1986 Midwest Herpetological Seminar*.

Eunectes murinus Anaconda

Size: potentially to 900 cm (360 in)
Range: South America

The anaconda is arguably the world's largest snake. Its enormous girth can accommodate large mammals up to the size of deer and sheep, and its diet in the wild apparently extends to crocodilians. The head is long and narrow, barely wider than the neck. The ground colour is olive green, with dark blotches along the back, and smaller, light-centred dark blotches along the flanks.

This species is hardly suitable for private collections on account of its size. However, it has obvious attractions for zoological gardens and for the few collectors with both the dedication and the space to cater for and accommodate such an enormous serpent. Needless to say, it requires a very large cage, in effect, a small room, fitted out with a stout branch or tree-trunk on which the snake will climb. A large water bowl or, preferably, a built-in pool with a drain, is essential as this snake is semi-aquatic and spends much of its time submerged. A temperature of 25–32°C (77–90°F) is required, and the species will usually take food readily, although it will often feed only at night. The diet can consist of almost any species of mammal of suitable size, as well as chickens, but individuals often have preferences. Beware that even half-grown anacondas are powerful snakes and can be aggressive – handling should never be undertaken lightly.

Although captive breeding has been achieved on more than one occasion, the factors which induce this are not well defined. Maturity appears to be attained at a length of about 250 cm (100 in), which can be reached in less than six years.

Breeding data (from literature and P. Strimple)

Time of mating:	April–May
Gestation period:	210–240 days
Litter size:	14–18 (average of 3 litters, 16)
Mortality rate:	No records of stillbirths
Size of neonates:	75–81 cm (30–32 in)
First food:	Young mice and rats (these may be taken before the initial shed of the young, which can be delayed for up to 81 days)

KEY REFERENCE:

Strimple, P. (1986). 'Captive propagation of the green anaconda, *Eunectes murinus murinus*'. 'The Forked tongue' (*Journal of the Greater Cincinnati Herpetological Society*), 11(6):5–9.

Eunectes notaeus   Yellow Anaconda (Plate 10)

Size: to 300 cm (120 in), occasionally larger
Range: South America

A pale brown or yellowish snake with large black blotches along its back. The blotches on its flanks are smaller and lack the light centres which distinguish it from the previous species. In habits, this species is similar to its larger relative, but is, if anything, more aquatic.

10. Yellow Anaconda, *Eunectes notaeus*, a smaller form than its better-known congener, and thus more easily catered for, although this species is also aggressive. It has been bred in captivity on a number of occasions.

11. Mexican Rosy Boa, *Lichanura trivirgata trivirgata*.

In captivity, its requirements are similar to those of the anaconda, but it is more resistant to cold than that species. Mating may be induced by a temperature drop of about 5°C (9°F) during the winter.

Breeding data (from literature)

Time of mating:	October–December
Gestation period:	225–270 days
Litter size:	5–19 (average of 11 clutches, 10.6)
Mortality rate:	Stillborn young have been reported, though rarely
Size of neonates:	38–65 cm (15–26 in)
First food:	Mice, fish

KEY REFERENCE:

Townson, S. (1985). 'The captive reproduction and growth of the yellow anaconda, *Eunectes notaeus*.' In: *Reptiles; Breeding, Behaviour and Veterinary Aspects*, Townson, S. and Lawrence, K. (eds). British Herpetological Society, London.

Lichanura trivirgata   Rosy Boa (Plate 11 and Colour Plate 6)

Size:	to about 100 cm (40 in)
Range:	extreme south-western North America (California, Arizona) and adjacent parts of Mexico

The rosy boa is a stout species with a small head and small shiny scales. The ground colour is usually slate-grey or brown, and this is broken by three broad longitudinal stripes which vary in colour according to subspecies: those of the Mexican subspecies, *L. t. trivirgata*, are deep chocolate brown, contrasting strongly with the ground colour which tends to be pale, often creamy; those of the coastal rosy boa, *L. t. roseofusca*, are commonly reddish-brown with irregular borders; and those of the desert rosy boa, *L. t. gracia*, are pink, orange or tan with well-defined edges. (Note that the taxonomy of these subspecies is currently under review.)

The rosy boa, in all of its forms, makes a good subject for captive breeding. It requires a medium-sized cage with a hide-box and water bowl. This species rarely if ever climbs and so the cage need not be high. The food consists of mice of appropriate size, bearing in mind that the species has a fairly small gape and will not take proportionately large prey; weaning mice are about right for adult snakes. During the summer, a temperature of 25–30°C (77–86°F) should be maintained, although this may be allowed to fall slightly during the night. In order to induce breeding, the temperature should be reduced to about 12°C (53°F) for at least two months in the winter. Animals of 60 cm (24 in) are sexually mature and this size can be reached in less than two years.

Availability: Rosy boas are protected throughout their range, but enough individuals are in collections to ensure a small but regular supply of captive-bred young.

Breeding data (from literature and L. Rouch)

Time of mating:	March–July
Gestation period:	103–134 days
Litter size:	3–6 (average of 18 litters, 4.2)
Mortality rate:	No stillbirths recorded
Size of neonates:	27–36 cm (11–14 in)
First food:	Pink mice

Sanzinia madagascariensis Madagascan Tree Boa

Size: to 250 cm (100 in)
Range: Madagascar

A semi-arboreal boa which is usually greenish with dark triangular blotches on the flanks, the apices of which sometimes meet across the dorsal mid-line. Light-coloured scales may be grouped irregularly within the dark triangles, and a wide dark line runs from the eye to the angle of the jaw. Individuals from certain areas of northern Madagascar are yellowish, and the offspring of these specimens are also yellow, as opposed to the brick-red coloration of normal young.

This species is not among the easiest boas to keep and breed. It requires a medium-sized cage, which should be high and contain a forked bough for climbing and resting on. Food consists of mice, although some specimens will only take birds, e.g. quail, finches, etc. A temperature of about 30°C (86°F) is required and it seems likely that mating takes place in response to a slight lowering of this, although hard data is lacking. The young may require force-feeding.

Breeding data (from literature)

Time of mating:	Not known, births recorded December–March from females which were pregnant when captured
Gestation period:	Not known, but at least 240 days
Litter size:	1–13 (average of 8 litters, 8.9)

Mortality rate:	12.3% stillbirths are reported overall
Size of neonates:	40–45 cm (16–18 in)
First food:	Half-grown mice, but may require force-feeding

KEY REFERENCES:

Branch, W. R. and Erasmus, H. (1976). Reproduction in Madagascar ground and tree boas. *Int. Zoo Yb.* Vol 16:78–80.

Foekema, G. M. M. (1971). 'Vijf geboorten bij *Sanzina madagascariensis*'. In two parts: *Lacerta* 29(4):43–48 and *Lacerta* 29(5):51–57. (In Dutch with an English summary.)

Subfamilies Pythoninae, Calabarinae and Loxoceminae – Pythons

The three subfamilies whose members are popularly known as 'pythons' are widely divergent groups of animals. The Pythoninae contains a number of medium to large-sized snakes, all restricted to the Old World – Africa, Asia and Australasia. The Calabarinae contain a single, small burrowing species from West Africa. Similarly, the Loxoceminae contains but a single species, also a small burrowing species but found, in this case, in the New World, in fact restricted to a small part of Mexico.

Care of the pythons, like that of the boas, depends greatly upon the size of the species concerned. However, the most commonly kept species tend to be hardier, in my experience, than the boas. Breeding these species varies from easy and straightforward to all but impossible (at present).

Gravid females of some species habitually bask with their ventral surfaces uppermost, or at least partially turned over. This behaviour is obviously associated with thermoregulation of the developing eggs, and should be regarded as normal. A further peculiarity of several species is the habit of brooding the eggs. Females of these species coil around the eggs as soon as they are laid, pushing them into a pyramidal heap as they do so. They remain in this position throughout the incubation period, rarely leaving the clutch, even to eat or drink. There is conflicting evidence as to the purpose of this behaviour; some species appear to be able to raise the temperature of their eggs slightly by producing a small amount of metabolic heat, accompanied by rhythmic twitching movements, whereas observations on other species have provided no evidence that this takes place. It seems likely that the prime purpose of brooding is to disguise the clutch which, consisting as it does of large white eggs, would otherwise be conspicuous and vulnerable to predation. In addition, the presence of the female undoubtedly deters all but the most determined predators.

Those species which naturally brood their eggs may be allowed to do so in captivity. If the cage is large, the female will choose the most suitable area for laying, and subsequent care consists of spraying the clutch occasionally in order to prevent the eggs from drying out. Alternatively, the female may be placed in a special container for egg-laying, consisting of a large box (wood or styrofoam has been used), lined with heat-tape to give the correct temperature of about 30°C (86°F). Under these conditions humidity can be maintained more easily, and the female benefits from the security of an enclosed site. In order to facilitate the maintenance of high humidity, it is advantageous to place a layer of sphagnum moss (or absorbent cloth) on the bottom of the box. Further details are given where necessary in the species accounts.

Aspidites melanocephalus   Black-headed Python

    Size: to 200 cm (80 in), occasionally larger
    Range: Australia

A bronze, tan or brown snake with numerous narrow, darker crossbands along its back. The head and throat are jet black.

This species is not commonly kept in captivity due to problems in obtaining specimens. Although it appears to eat mainly snakes in the wild, it usually adapts well to a diet of rodents. It has been known to eat members of its own species, and specimens should therefore be kept in solitary confinement except when matings are attempted, at which time the snakes should be carefully watched. A temperature of 25–30°C (77–86°F) is required, although it is not known whether this needs to be adjusted in order to induce mating. At the Dallas Zoo matings occurred during the two months immediately following a period during which the animals were sprayed with water every week for four months. Females of this species normally brood their eggs but in all reported cases of captive breeding they were removed and incubated artificially.

Availability: Hardly ever available outside Australia, although small numbers are maintained by a few zoological gardens and specialist (and wealthy) collectors.

Breeding data (from literature)

Time of mating:	June onwards
Mating–egg-laying:	Not known
Number of eggs:	5–12 (average 8.5)
Incubation period:	65–93 days
Hatch-rate:	Not known

Size of hatchlings: 66–70 cm (26–27½ in)
First food: Young mice

KEY REFERENCES:

Barker, D. G. (1981). 'Maintenance and breeding of pythons at the Dallas Zoo'. *Proc. 5th Ann. Symp. on Captive Propagation and Husbandry* 86–92.

Charles, N., Field, R., and Shine, R. (1985). 'Notes on the reproductive biology of Australian pythons, genera *Aspidites*, *Liasis* and *Morelia*.' *Herp. Review* 16(2):45–48.

Calabaria reinwardtii   Calabar Ground Python

Size: to 100 cm (40 in)
Range: West Africa

Calabaria is a cylindrical, blunt-tailed python with small eyes. It varies from brown or black with irregular blotches of dirty white, yellow or red. Well-marked individuals are very colourful.

This is a highly fossorial python, spending much of its time beneath the surface of the soil or among leaf-litter. It probably feeds mostly on nestling rodents, which it hunts by entering their burrows. In captivity, therefore, it requires a deep substrate of leaf-litter or wood-shavings. In addition, a hide-box should be provided in which the food is placed in order to allow the snake to feed in a confined space. A temperature of 25–30°C (77–86°F) is recommended, and it may be advantageous to maintain the humidity fairly high, say above 50%, although precise data is lacking.

Availability: This species is imported fairly regularly from West Africa. The Calabar ground python appears never to have been bred in captivity, although females which were gravid when imported have laid small clutches of eggs, none of which have hatched.

Chondropython viridis   Green Tree Python (Plate 12 and Colour Plate 7)

Size: to about 150 cm (60 in), occasionally larger
Range: Papua New Guinea, extreme northern Australia (Queensland)

An extremely beautiful serpent, possibly the most desirable snake of all. Adults are pure bright green except for a row of irregular white markings distributed along the dorsal mid-line. Juveniles are dimorphic and may be bright sulphur yellow or brick-red, and also show the same white markings which they will retain into adulthood. Very occasionally, colour

81

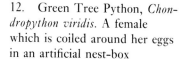

12. Green Tree Python, *Chondropython viridis*. A female which is coiled around her eggs in an artificial nest-box

mutants crop up in which the green colour is replaced by bright sky blue, due to the lack of yellow pigment in the upper layers of the skin. Although this species may be aggressive at first, its general disposition is usually better than that of the almost identical species, *Corallus canina*.

In captivity this highly arboreal species requires a tall cage with at least one branch arranged in a horizontal position. A water bowl may be included, but the snakes will usually prefer to drink water that has collected in their coils after spraying, which should be carried out daily. Most specimens will eat mice or small rats readily, although hatchlings often require force-feeding at first. In all cases it is advisable to offer food with tongs since this species rarely comes down onto the ground to feed. Temperature should be about 30°C (86°F) during the day, lower, about 25°C (77°F) during the night, and humidity should be between 50% and 100% throughout (if a large water container is placed in the cage, the higher daytime temperature will automatically raise the humidity at this time, but regular spraying is still recommended). On no account should ventilation be decreased in order to save on the amount of spraying necessary, with the possible exception of a few days at a time when it is hoped to stimulate mating. During the winter, the night-time temperature should be allowed to fall to 20°C (68°F) or slightly less in order to improve breeding results. However, it appears likely that relative humidity is of more importance in inducing the snakes to mate than is temperature, or possibly a combination of the two factors is necessary.

After mating, females should be allowed to maintain a high body temperature throughout the day and night, and this is best achieved by supplementing the normal heating arrangements with one or two red light bulbs switched on permanently, beneath which the females will bask. There is some difference of opinion as to whether the eggs should be removed from the female to be incubated artificially, or whether she should be allowed to brood them. Either way, results until now have been disappointing, with a high proportion of the eggs failing to hatch, either through infertility or through poor development. If the female is to be left with her eggs, some arrangement must be made to enable her to lay them in a secluded part of the cage. The system used with a fair degree of success by Mike Nolan of London was to attach a 'nest-box' to the outside of the cage, connected to it by a small opening. The top of the nest-box was hinged so that the female and eggs could be inspected, and in order to introduce water. A layer of moisture-retaining material, such as sphagnum moss, should be placed in the bottom of the box so that a high humidity can be maintained throughout the incubation.

Availability: Although breeding this species has so far proved to be anything but straightforward, useful data is accumulating and it should not be too long before supplies of captive-bred animals become more reliable; there is an undoubted demand for high quality, parasite-free hatchlings.

Breeding data (from literature)

Time of mating:	January–March, July–September
Mating–egg-laying:	76–113 days
Number of eggs:	10–25 (average of 17 clutches, 16.4) including a high proportion of infertile eggs
Incubation period:	47–70 days, typically 50–53 days at 30°C (86°F)
Hatch-rate:	Poor, only about 50% of fertile eggs overall
Size of hatchlings:	25–30 cm (10–12 in)
First food:	Small mice, but force-feeding often required

KEY REFERENCES:

Gray, P. (1977). 'A captive breeding of the green tree python, *Chondropython viridis*'. *Proc. 2nd Ann. Symp. on Captive Propagation and Husbandry*, 34–38.

Walsh, T. (1977). 'Husbandry and breeding of *Chondropython viridis*'. *Natl. Assoc. for Sound Wildlife Programs*, 1(2):10–22.

Walsh, T. (1979). 'Further notes on the husbandry, breeding and behaviour of *Chondropython viridis*'. *Proc. 3rd Ann. Symp. on Captive Propagation and Husbandry*, 102–111.

Liasis albertisi   D'Alberti's Python, White-lipped Python

Size: to about 200 cm (80 in)
Range: Australia, New Guinea, islands in the Torres Straits

Australian specimens are brown or grey-brown with cream lips. Specimens from northern New Guinea are bronze with jet black heads and cream or white lips. There are no body markings, but the entire snake is highly iridescent.

Information on the care of this species is scanty. Furthermore, there is some confusion as to whether or not the two forms constitute a single species or two closely related forms, in which case the small amount of data which is available may be a composite of the two (*L. albertisi* and *L. mackloti*). They appear to require a temperature in the region of 30°C (86°F) and feed readily on young rats. Mating may be stimulated by lowering the temperature to about 20°C (68°F) but this species is aggressive and temperamental in captivity and breeding has not proved easy.

Availability: This species is totally protected, and it is likely to be some time before a supply of captive-bred animals is freely available.

Breeding data (from literature)

Time of mating:	June, September–November
Mating–egg-laying:	49–60 days
Number of eggs:	7–17 (average of 6 clutches, 12.1)
Incubation period:	56–69 days (average of 3 clutches, 11.3)
Hatch-rate:	About 50%
Size of hatchlings:	25–30 cm (10–12 in)
First food:	Pink mice, but apparently only when placed on a damp substrate

KEY REFERENCE:
Sipperley, G. (1986). 'The white-lipped python, *Liasis albertisi*'. *San Diego Herp. Soc. Newsletter* 8(12):1–2.
Ross, R. and Larman, R. (1977). 'Captive breeding in two species of python, *Liasis albertisis* and *L. mackloti*'. *Int. Zoo Yb.* Vol 17:133–136.

Liasis childreni   Children's Python

Size: to about 100 cm (40 in)
Range: northern two-thirds of Australia

Children's python, one of the smallest species in the subfamily, is a relatively slender species marked with dark brown mottlings (sometimes arranged into indistinct crossbars) on a paler brown ground, fading to cream on the flanks and ventral surface.

This species has turned out to be one of the easiest in the group to keep and breed. In all respects it may be treated as a subtropical colubrid, i.e. given a medium-sized cage with hide-box and water bowl, a temperature of 25–30°C (77–86°F), and a diet of mice. Breeding is induced by cooling the adults to about 15°C (59°F) for two or three months in the winter, during which time they will mate readily. Although the females normally brood their eggs, most breeders favour artificial incubation. The young grow quickly and may mature in eighteen months.

Availability: Supplies of this species have steadily improved over the last few years as breeders have increased their output, and prices have lowered accordingly.

Breeding data (from literature)

Time of mating:	September–February
Mating–egg-laying:	160 days
Number of eggs:	3–14 (average of 9 clutches, 9.6)
Incubation period:	51–66 days
Hatch-rate:	Above 75%
Size of hatchlings:	21–27 cm ($8\frac{1}{2}$–$10\frac{1}{2}$ in)
First food:	Pink mice

KEY REFERENCES:

Chiras, S. (1982). 'Captive reproduction of the Children's python, *Liasis childreni*'. *Herp. Review* 13(1):14–15.

McLain, J. M. (1980). 'Reproduction in captive Children's pythons, *Liasis childreni*'. *Proc. 4th. Ann. Symp. on Captive Propagation and Husbandry*, 79–82.

Ross, R. A. (1973). 'Successful mating and hatching of Children's python, *Liasis childreni*'. HISS-NJ 1(6):181–182.

Loxocemus bicolor   Mexican Dwarf Python (Plate 13)

Size: to about 100 cm (40 in)
Range: Eastern Mexico and Costa Rica

This strange python is uniformly brown dorsally, save for a few scattered patches, each consisting of a group of white scales. The whole animal is highly iridescent when viewed in a bright light.

Little is known about the natural history of this rare python. In captivity it does very well if supplied with a cage containing several inches of substrate, e.g. wood-shavings. Temperatures should be 25–30°C (77–

13. Mexican Dwarf Python, *Loxocemus bicolor*, a little-known python from Central America, which adapts to captivity well but has not yet been bred.

86°F) and the diet consists of small rodents. To my knowledge, the species has never been bred in captivity, the main reason probably being that, due to its scarcity, few collectors have managed to put together a male and a female.

Python amethystinus Amethystine Python

>   Size: normally to 400 cm (160 in) but potentially to 850 cm (340 in)
>   Range: extreme northern Australia

This species is Australia's largest snake. It is pale to olive-brown with many darker transverse bars arranged randomly along the back. The head is normally unmarked, and the whole body is iridescent.

Although the species is sometimes displayed in zoological gardens, it seems to have been bred only rarely outside Australia. Its general care consists of a large cage with the usual stout branch and large water bowl or pool. A diet of rodents or larger mammals is necessary and the temperature should be maintained at about 25–30°C (77–86°F). It appears to be especially prone to parasite infestations and bacterial diseases, and this may account for its poor record. Despite their large potential size, adults mature at less than 300 cm (120 in).

Three clutches have been recorded, two of 7 eggs and one of 12. These hatched after a period of 78–107 days and the hatchlings measured

61–66 cm (24–26 in) in length. Females of this species normally brood their eggs; both artificial and natural incubations appear to have been used successfully in captive breeding.

Availability: This species is hardly ever available.

Similar species: The recently described *Python oenpelliensis*, is closely related to the amethystine python and its maintenance will probably be similar. Only a single case of egg-laying (from a wild-caught female) is reported, in which 10 eggs were laid but failed to hatch.

KEY REFERENCE:

Charles, N., Field, R., and Shine, R. (1985). 'Notes on the reproductive biology of Australian pythons, genera *Aspidites*, *Liasis*, and *Morelia*'. *Herp. Review* 16(2):45–48.

Python anchietae   Angolan Python

An exceedingly rare dwarf python from West Africa, *P. achietae* is superficially quite similar to the royal python (*see* page XX), but more slender. It measures little over 100 cm (40 in) in length, and is reddish-brown with black-edged white spots and bands.

Only a single report of breeding this python has been found, from a wild mating. A clutch of 5 eggs was laid, 4 of which hatched after 72–75 days at approximately 28°C (8°F).

KEY REFERENCE:

Patterson, R. W. (1978). 'Hatching of Anchieta's dwarf python'. *Int. Zoo. Yb.* 18:99–101.

Python curtus   Blood Python

Size: to 200 cm (80 in)
Range: Malaysia, Sumatra and Borneo

A short, stout-bodied python with variable coloration. Many specimens are grey or brown with irregular darker stripes and blotches on the back and flanks. A dark line joins the eye to the angle of the jaw, and another runs down the centre of the head, between the eyes. However, the most attractive specimens, which apparently originate in Sumatra, are suffused entirely with brick-red or carmine.

The care of this species is one of the most frustrating experiences in snake-keeping. Very few specimens feed at all, and those that do, feed only infrequently and fail to thrive for any length of time. Although the solution is by no means cut and dried, it appears that this snake requires a high humidity at all times, being associated with swampy and other damp habitats in the wild. A large water bowl is essential so that the animal can submerge itself completely. Furthermore, a constant high temperature, in the region of 30–32°C (86–90°F) is necessary. Under these conditions, however, blood pythons lose their tractability and become aggressive! It is worth noting in this respect that several specimens housed in very basic cages at the Kuala Lumpur Zoo, a region of oppressively high humidity, took food greedily and were certainly very aggressive. The diet of this species consists of rodents and birds such as quail and pigeons, and these are usually taken at night.

Additional problems may be the result of heavy parasite burdens which accompany freshly caught wild specimens, and prophylactic treatment for intestinal worms and protozoans is advised. This species is rarely bred in captivity, but clutches of 10–16 eggs have been recorded, which take 58–92 days to hatch at 30–32°C (86–90°F). Females of this species normally brood their eggs, but make unreliable mothers in captivity. The young measure 30–45 cm (12–18 in).

Availability: Wild-caught specimens are available from time to time, but do not adapt to captivity easily for the reasons given above. Young specimens, when available, may be a better proposition, but captive-bred stock is rarely offered.

Python molurus Burmese Python, Indian Python (Colour Plate 8)

> Size: to 650 cm (260 in)
> Range: Southern Asia

Two subspecies are recognised. The nominate one, *P. m. molurus*, the Indian python, usually referred to as 'light phase', has a cream or buff ground colour with large brown blotches on the back and flanks. Although irregular in shape, these interlock to some extent, producing a 'giraffe-like' pattern. A characteristic arrowhead marking begins on the neck and finishes between, or just forward of, the eyes. The Burmese python (or 'dark phase' Indian python), *P. m. bivittatus* is marked in exactly the same way, except that both the ground colour and the blotches are darker, deep chestnut brown on yellow, fading to cream on the flanks. A further subspecies, *P. m. pimbura*, was recognised until recently. This name was given to specimens originating in Sri Lanka (Ceylon), but these are now considered to be *P. m. molurus*. It appears that most of the 'light phase' Indian pythons in captivity originated from this region.

In contrast to the previous species, the Indian python is among the most adaptable and accommodating snakes to keep in captivity, the only problem associated with it being that of its enormous size. Adults obviously require a large cage, and this should be heated to 25–30°C (77–86°F). It will eat a range of warm-blooded prey, depending on size, including mice, rats, rabbits and chickens, and young animals will grow at an alarming rate if fed ad lib. Note that hatchlings which are fed entirely on chicks grow into unsatisfactory adults, with poor muscle tone, and will be unlikely to breed successfully. Their diet should therefore consist of at least 50% rodents.

Breeding of this species has been achieved very many times. Adults mate during the winter, while the temperature is a few degrees lower than normal, and the females brood their eggs, this being one of the few species where there is evidence that the temperature of the eggs is raised slightly (or at least, stabilised) by the twitching activities of the mother. Although the eggs can be removed for artificial incubation, there is normally no advantage to this, and in doing so the keeper is depriving himself of the opportunity to observe an interesting aspect of snake reproductive behaviour. Males mature by the time they reach 300 cm (120 in) and females at 400 cm (160 in), which can occur in less than three years.

Availability: Dark phase Indian pythons are readily available, most as captive-bred hatchlings. Adults are also frequently offered at low prices as they often outgrow their accommodation, making urgent disposal necessary. Light phase animals are nowhere near as easy to come by and, furthermore, due to difficulty in obtaining mates for single animals of this subspecies, they have frequently been hybridised with the commoner form. After several generations of breeding, animals from these impure strains can be difficult to identify.

Breeding data (from literature)

Time of mating:	January–March
Mating–egg-laying:	60–140 days
Number of eggs:	18–55 (average of 29 clutches, 35.9)*
Incubation period:	55–75 days
Hatch-rate:	Highly variable, from total losses to 100%
Size of hatchlings:	About 55 cm (22 in)
First food:	Mice, small rats

*clutches of the Burmese python, *P. m. molurus*, tend, on average, to be smaller.

KEY REFERENCE:

Townson, S. (1980). 'Observations of the reproduction of the Indian python in captivity, with special reference to the interbreeding of the two subspecies, *Python molurus molurus* and *Python molurus bivittatus*'. In: Townson, S. et al (eds), *The Care and Breeding of Captive Reptiles*, British Herpetological Society, London.

14. Royal Python, *Python regius* one of the most common species of python to obtain, but not among the easiest species to keep satisfactorily and therefore rarely bred.

Python regius Royal Python (Plate 14)

Size: to 120 cm (48 in), occasionally larger
Range: West Africa

The royal python, sometimes known as the ball python, is a short, stout species with a short tail. It is deep brown, almost black, with large irregular tan blotches which may have lighter edges. A tan line runs from the snout, through the eye to the angle of the jaw.

Being small and fairly inactive, this python needs only a medium-sized cage, with a low branch or stump for climbing on and a water bowl which is large enough for the animal to submerge itself completely. It requires a temperature of about 30°C (86°F), which should not normally be allowed to drop more than 5°C (9°F) at any time, although mating may only take place at periods when the temperature is allowed to fall to 23–25°C (73–77°F). Two problems associated with this species are its reluctance to feed and to breed. Many specimens go for several months before taking a single meal and, although this rarely does any permanent harm, it can be disconcerting. Some individuals have a preference for dead prey, whereas others will only take specific types of rodents, of which gerbils appear to be the favourite. Other than ensuring that the temperature is high enough, raising the humidity slightly and ensuring that a variety of prey animals is introduced at regular intervals, there is little that can be done to stimulate feeding; most specimens do eventually start to eat, although fasting may take place at intervals throughout the animal's life. Appetite stimulants, such as vitamin B12, have been used to good effect, but are probably unnecessary unless the animal begins to become emaciated, which usually does not occur for many months, often over one year.

Although this species has been widely kept, on account of its convenient size, attractive appearance and docility, it is very rarely bred. Such reports as there are suggest clutch sizes of 2–7 large eggs, laid at various times of the year, which hatch after 39–81 days (the reason for this discrepancy is not known, but is probably due to differences in temperature). Females brood their eggs, and may raise their temperature in doing so, but most clutches have been removed and incubated under artificial conditions. The young measure 38–43 cm (15–17 in) in length.

Availability: This species is widely available, regrettably only due to a continual influx of wild-caught animals, mostly destined for the pet trade, rather than the specialist market.

Python reticulatus   Reticulated Python

   Size: potentially to 900 cm (360 in) but usually smaller
   Range: South-east Asia

This giant snake is more slender than many pythons. Its ground colour is yellowish and the markings intricate, consisting of black blotches along the flanks, each one being adjacent to a black circular or ovoid marking. These often interconnect to form a lattice-like or reticulated pattern. In addition, patches of white scales are often present, especially in the black flank markings. The top of the head is unmarked, but a black line runs from the eye to the angle of the mouth. The head and body are strongly iridescent, especially under natural light.

This python is not one of the easiest or most pleasant to maintain. Apart from its huge size, problems stem from its belligerent disposition, few specimens ever becoming completely trustworthy. Nevertheless, it usually feeds readily, on a wide variety of mammals, dependent on size. It requires a temperature of 25–30°C (77–86°F), a large water bowl or pool and a sturdy branch, or rather tree trunk, on which to climb and rest. Animals mature at about 350 cm (140 in), and this species has been bred on more than one occasion, but few collectors have the facilities or inclination to attempt it. Mating takes place during the cooler months and up to 100, but more often 30–50, eggs are laid 100–150 days later. Females will brood their eggs, or they may be incubated artificially.

Hatching takes place about 60 days later, and the hatchlings measure 75–80 cm (30–32 in) in length. They will accept adult mice.

Availability: Reticulated pythons are imported from Asia in fairly large numbers, although their popularity is declining in favour of smaller, more manageable species. Captive-bred babies are unlikely ever to be generally available.

Python sebae   African Rock Python

Size: to about 600 cm (240 in)
Range: Southern and Central Africa

A large blotched python, being mid-brown with numerous irregular dark markings on the back and flanks. It could possibly be confused with the Indian python, but lacks the 'arrowhead' marking on the head of that species.

This species is not widely kept, except in Africa. It requires a large cage, with the usual water bowl and stout branch. It usually feeds readily, on rodents and larger mammals, according to size. Temperatures should be in the region of 25–30°C (77–86°F), but this is one of the hardiest of the giant snakes and will tolerate quite substantial temperature drops. It is unknown whether or not these are essential for breeding to take place, although it seems likely. In the northern hemisphere, eggs are laid from May to July, and from October to December in the southern hemisphere. The clutch may consist of up to 60 eggs and these are brooded by the female who, however, does not appear to influence their temperature. Incubation takes about 70–105 days and the hatchlings measure 45–55 cm (18–22 in) in length.

Availability: This species is protected and is therefore rarely offered. In addition, there appears to be little demand.

Python spilotes (= Morelia spilotes)   Carpet Python, Diamond Python (Plate 15)

Size: to 300 cm (120 in), occasionally larger
Range: Australia

The taxonomy of this species, like several of the Australian pythons, is chaotic. For the purposes of this book, two distinct forms or subspecies can be recognised, and are referred to by their 'traditional' names: *P. s. spilotes*, the diamond python, and *P. spilotes variegata*, the carpet python. All manner of other subspecific names have been assigned to various forms of these snakes, and some authorities recognise *P. variegata* as a distinct species.

15.   Diamond Python, *Python spilotes*, an attractive, but rarely available Australian species.

The diamond python, *P. s. spilotes*, which is the less commonly seen of the two forms, is basically a black snake with a pattern of small white specks over the entire body. Certain individuals have, in addition, a pattern of larger white spots arranged in poorly defined bars across the back and flanks. The carpet python, *P. s. variegata*, is a highly variable subspecies, according to its geographical origin (hence the confusion). The most common pattern is one of transverse bands, sometimes connected to form an irregular network. The ground colour and that of the markings may be light and dark grey, yellow or gold on dark grey or brown, or buff on brown or reddish-brown. Every conceivable inter-mediate arrangement may also be found. Irrespective of the actual colours and their arrangement, carpet pythons are invariably attractive and highly desirable snakes.

Their care in captivity is fairly straightforward. They require a medium to large cage and a temperature of 25–30°C (77–86°F). They like to climb, and a stout branch should also be included, along with a hide-box. Food is rodents, which are usually taken without any problem. Breeding appears to be initiated by a lowering of the temperature during the winter. Females will brood their own eggs if allowed to do so, although successful breeding has also occurred by means of artificial incubation.

Availability: This species is totally protected, but is fairly widely bred. Therefore a good supply of captive-bred animals exists, although the variation in markings would make prior inspection advantageous, wherever possible.

Breeding data (from literature)

Timing of mating:	January–February, August–September
Mating to egg-laying:	Not known
Number of eggs:	9–54 (average of 22 clutches, 21.1)
Incubation period:	54–65 days, typically 64 days at 28°C (82°F)
Hatch-rate:	60–70%
Size of hatchlings:	40–51 cm (16–20 in)
First food:	Young mice

KEY REFERENCE:

Charles, N., Field, R., and Shine, R. (1985). 'Notes on the reproductive biology of Australian pythons, genera *Aspidites liasis*, and *Morelia*'. *Herp. Review* 16(2):45–48.

Other species: At present, there is a great deal of interest in pythons from the Indonesian and South Pacific regions. Species such as *Python timoriensis* and *P. boeleni* are highly sought after and will undoubtedly be bred in the near future. However, there is insufficient data available at this time to give accounts of these interesting snakes.

CHAPTER 8

Genus *Lampropeltis* – Kingsnakes

The kingsnakes, genus *Lampropeltis*, are deservedly among the most popular with snake-keepers and are collectively among the most frequently bred. For our purposes, the genus falls into three fairly natural groups: the prairie kingsnake, *Lampropeltis calligaster*, is a blotched brown snake; the various forms of the common kingsnake, *Lampropeltis getulus*, have markings consisting of black and white or black and yellow in various different arrangements; and the so-called tri-coloured kingsnakes, of which there are several species, have red, black and white bands arranged into a series of triads around the body.

All kingsnakes are medium-sized, cylindrical snakes with smooth, shiny scales. All species either constrict their prey or immobilise it by pressing it against a solid surface, and many species have a wide range of prey which includes rodents, lizards and other snakes. All species are secretive by nature and several of them, e.g. *L. alterna*, appear to spend the greater part of their lives in underground fissures and chambers, rarely venturing out onto the surface except to find mates during the breeding season.

In captivity they require a medium-sized cage, which need not be especially high since they rarely climb. Owing to their secretive habits, a hide-box is essential, unless the cage is of the drawer-type (which is ideally suited to these species). Temperatures vary with the species, but the montane species at least require a cool spell of two to three months if they are to breed. In captivity, most species take mice readily, although hatchlings of several of the smaller species prefer lizards and may require force-feeding at first.

Lampropeltis calligaster   Prairie Kingsnake (Plate 16)

    Size: to 100 cm (40 in)
    Range: South-eastern North America

16. Prairie Kingsnake, *Lampropeltis calligaster calligaster*, a species which breeds readily in captivity and of which an albino strain is also available.

The most commonly kept subspecies, *L. c. calligaster*, is a brown or grey snake, with about 60 dark brown blotches or saddles along the back, alternating with smaller blotches along each flank. A dark phase exists, in which the markings are obscure. One other subspecies, *L. c. rhombomaculata*, the mole snake, is rarely seen in captivity. The markings of this form are smaller and less distinct, and many specimens become almost uniformly brown as they mature. The care of both species is identical, although there is little breeding information on the mole snake.

The prairie kingsnake is among the easiest snakes to keep and breed. It prefers a temperature around 25°C (77°F), and the usual hide-box, etc. Food consists of mice, the hatchlings almost always accepting pinkies without problems. Breeding size is reached in the second year and adults should be cooled to around 12–15°C (53–59°F) for two to three months in the winter.

Availability: Captive-bred *L. c. calligaster* are readily available, including an amelanistic form, but captive-bred *L. c. rhombomaculata* do not appear to be available.

Breeding data (from literature, R. Applegate, H. Cohen, V. Scheidt)
      Time of mating: March–April
Mating to egg-laying: 43–55 days

Number of eggs:	5–16 (average 9.0 from 17 clutches)
Incubation period:	50–60 days, typically 59 days at 28°C (82°F)
Success rate:	Usually high, 90% +
Size of hatchlings:	30 cm (12 in)
First food:	Pink mice

KEY REFERENCE:

Coote, J. (1981). 'Second generation captive breeding of the prairie kingsnake, *Lampropeltis calligaster calligaster*'. *Proc. Sixth Symposium of the Association of British Wild Animal Keepers*.

Lampropeltis getulus   Common Kingsnake

Size:	to about 120 cm (48 in)
Range:	most of North and Central America

The 'common' kingsnake occurs in a number of distinct subspecies. Since these are avidly collected by snake-keepers, they are described separately below. Care of all subspecies, however, is similar. They require a temperature of 25–30°C (77–86°F), and a diet consisting entirely of mice of appropriate size. Because they regularly eat other snakes they should not be kept with other species under any circumstances and, furthermore, the young should be housed individually at all times. Adults of similar size may be housed together, e.g. during the breeding season, but should be carefully watched during feeding sessions. The young grow quickly with adequate feeding and reach breeding size in their second summer. Breeding is straightforward and easy; the adults should be cooled to 15–20°C (59–68°F) for a minimum of two to three months during the winter.

Breeding data (from literature, R. Applegate, H. Cohen, V. Scheidt)

Time of mating:	March–June
Mating to egg-laying:	31–49 days (second clutches are frequently recorded, appearing during late summer after a further mating)
Number of eggs:	3–21 (average of 73 clutches from 8 subspecies, 9.3)
Incubation period:	47–70 days
Hatch rate:	High, usually more than 90%. (Twins have been recorded for *L. g. niger*.)
Size of young:	24–33 cm ($9\frac{1}{2}$–13 in)
First food:	Pink mice taken with no problems

THE SUBSPECIES ARE:

L. g. californiae   Californian Kingsnake (Plate 17 and Colour Plates 9 and 10)

This subspecies exists in a variety of forms. Typical individuals are black or brown with 21–44 white, cream or yellow bands encircling the body. Usually, examples from desert areas are jet black and pure white, and eagerly sought after, whereas coastal forms are brown and yellow or brown and cream. In addition, a proportion of the individuals from the San Diego region have a single white stripe running longitudinally down the back, with a less distinct white stripe on each flank. Both striped and banded forms may hatch from a single clutch of eggs, but matings between striped individuals and banded animals from other parts of the range produce young with an irregular mishmash of stripes and bands, sometimes known as 'dot-dash' kingsnakes.

Availability: Captive-bred striped and banded Californian kingsnakes are readily available, in both normal and albino forms. However, the sale of native species is illegal in California and so only mutant forms are available here.

L. g. floridana   Florida Kingsnake

A brownish kingsnake with a varying amount of yellow or cream on each scale. Scales with large areas of yellow are often arranged into a series of crossbands so that the overall appearance is of an indistinctly blotched snake.

Availability: Florida kingsnakes are not bred as frequently as several of the other subspecies, but captive-bred young are available from time to time. Wild-caught animals also become available, but are usually inferior in health and appearance.

L. g. getulus   Eastern Kingsnake, Chain Kingsnake

Dark brown or black with narrow white crossbars, each of which divides into two on the flanks. The 'arms' of each band connect with those of the neighbouring band to form a series of links along the length of the snake. Note: this subspecies tends to have larger clutches than average.

Availability: Eastern kingsnakes are rarely bred in captivity, although wild-caught animals are sometimes available.

L. g. holbrooki   Speckled Kingsnake

Black or dark brown with a yellow or cream spot on the centre of each scale. In the best examples, the speckling is evenly distributed over the

17. Californian Kingsnake, *Lampropeltis getulus californiae*, an albino example of the striped phase (see also Colour Plate 10).

entire body, but this form intergrades with several of its neighbouring subspecies and traces of bands or blotches are sometimes visible. Speckled kingsnakes are unusual among this species in being aggressive by nature, although captive-bred animals rarely present problems.

Availability: Speckled kingsnakes are frequently bred, although mainly in their albino form; normally marked (heterozygous) offspring are frequently offered for sale.

L. g. niger Black Kingsnake

This subspecies is like a chain kingsnake but with the white markings reduced and less distinct. Some individuals may be almost totally black.

Availability: Rarely available, either as wild-caught or captive-bred.

L. g. nigritus Mexican Black Kingsnake

The pure form is completely jet black when adult, although hatchlings may show traces of markings similar to those of the desert kingsnake (*see* below), and these sometimes persist in animals which originate in areas where the two subspecies intergrade. *Nigritus* differs from the preceding subspecies in having a solid black underside.

99

Availability: The Mexican black kingsnake is bred in fairly large numbers. Strains vary in the degree to which markings are retained, and the only way to be sure of their potential is to examine the parents.

L. g. splendida   Desert Kingsnake (Colour Plate 11)

Black, with certain scales having a yellow centre. These are arranged along the flanks and into several crossbands: the overall impression is of a speckled kingsnake with 50–90 solid black blotches down the back. In specimens from southern Arizona and New Mexico, the marked scales are spotted with pure white, increasing the contrast between the blotches and the ground colour: these attractive animals are possibly intergrades between *splendida* and *nigritus*.

Availability: The desert kingsnake is not bred as often as it deserves, although captive-bred young are occasionally available. Wild-caught animals are frequently offered, but the subspecies is so variable that it is unwise to buy unseen.

L. g. 'yumensis'   Yuma Kingsnake

This form, which, according to most authorities, is no longer a valid subspecies, is similar to the black and white 'desert phase' of the Californian kingsnake, save that the scales comprising the white bands have brown on their bases. It appears to be an intergrade between *californiae* and *nigritus*, but may occasionally be found listed.

Availability: Animals listed as 'desert phase' Californian kingsnakes may be of this form.

Tri-coloured Kingsnakes and Milk Snakes

At present, six species and numerous subspecies of *Lampropeltis* are included in this group. All are attractive snakes and the various forms provide ample scope for the collector, and many specialise entirely in them. Unfortunately, their taxonomy is in a state of chaos, with new subspecies appearing frequently, sometimes to be invalidated almost immediately. Other forms are regarded as full species by some but as subspecies by others. The following arrangement is fairly conservative: it is not necessarily scientifically accurate but lists the species under the names by which they are most commonly advertised. The difference between many of the subspecies is slight, to say the least, and the possibility of hybridisation between closely related forms, either deliberate or accidental, is ever present. In addition, several forms are highly variable and exist in a number of distinct 'phases'; the only sure way of knowing what you are getting is to inspect both the offspring and their parents before buying. If this is not possible, buy from a breeder who specialises in these snakes, and who should be able to guarantee their genetic integrity.

With the exception of some of the *L. triangulum* group, all these species are highland forms. It would appear that a period of hibernation is *essential* if breeding is to take place. Other than this, care of tri-coloured kingsnakes is fairly straightforward. They require small to medium-sized cages with a hide-box or, preferably, a drawer. Food consists mainly of small rodents, although some species much prefer lizards, especially as juveniles. They have fairly small mouths and their prey should be graded to take this into account: many cases of snakes refusing to feed stem from offering food items which are too large.

KEY REFERENCES:

Tryon, B. W. and Murphy, J. B. (1982). 'Miscellaneous notes on the reproductive biology of reptiles. 5. Thirteen varieties of the genus *Lampropeltis*, species *mexicana*, *triangulum* and *zonata*'. *Transactions of the*

Kansas Academy of Sciences, 85(2):96–119.

Wagner, E. (1979). 'Breeding kingsnakes'. *Int. Zoo Yb.* 19:98–100.

Lampropeltis alterna   Grey-banded Kingsnake (Colour Plate 12)

Size: to about 100 cm (40 in)
Range: extreme southern Texas (Big Bend region) and adjacent areas
           of northern Mexico

Note: This snake was formerly known as *Lampropeltis mexicana alterna*, and will sometimes be found listed as such.

This species is incredibly variable – hardly any two are alike, even from the same clutch. Basically, two colour phases exist. Those known as 'Blair's' phase may be grey with orange saddles, the saddles being edged with a band of black scales and a narrow band of white. The orange saddles and the grey areas between them are broad, and typical examples have about fifteen saddles in all. The head is grey. These are sometimes known as 'light phase Blair's'. 'Dark phase Blair's' also have broad grey areas but no orange. Instead, the saddles are entirely black or dark grey except for the usual white edging. 'Alterna' phase animals are grey with narrow black bands, each band edged with white, and occasionally with a small area of orange in its centre. In addition, all possible variants between these extremes occur. Selective breeding over several generations should stabilise some of the more distinctive forms and the markings of offspring should become more predictable.

Care of the grey-banded kingsnake is as above. This species is among the most secretive of all snakes – its natural habitat consists of porous limestone hills and mountains, where it lives in deep crevices and fissures. Therefore it should be given ample hiding places, where it will spend the majority of its time. Otherwise, the only difficulty which may arise is in persuading the hatchlings to accept newborn mice: about 50% appear to do this without any trouble but the others will only take lizards. These will need to be persuaded to take mice by washing a pinkie and then transferring the smell of a lizard onto it. After a few such feeds, the snakes will normally accept pinkies without hesitation. Despite this slight drawback, the species is one of the most sought after of all the kingsnakes. Breeding presents little difficulty but the adults must be cooled to a maximum of 15°C (59°F) during the winter, otherwise only infertile eggs will be produced. Sexual maturity may be achieved within two years.

Availability: Grey-banded kingsnakes are bred in large numbers and will be found on most breeders' lists. As a result, their price, which was very high in the past, has now become more reasonable. Owing to variation in markings, buyers are advised to inspect the stock which they are planning to purchase.

Breeding data (from R. Applegate, H. Cohen, V. Scheidt)

Time of mating:	April–May
Mating–egg-laying:	29–59 days (second clutches are frequently recorded, in late summer)
Number of eggs:	5–14 (average of 17 clutches, 10.4)
Incubation period:	55–77 days
Hatch rate:	Usually high, over 75% (unless the adults are not cooled sufficiently during the winter)
Size of young:	25–27 cm (10–11 in)
First food:	Pink mice, lizards (*see* below)

KEY REFERENCE:

Tryon, B. W., and Murphy, J. B. (1982). 'Miscellaneous notes on the reproductive biology of reptiles. 5. Thirteen varieties of the genus *Lampropeltis*, species *mexicana*, *triangulum* and *zonata*'. *Transactions of the Kansas Academy of Sciences* 85(2):96–119.

Lampropeltis mexicana   Mexican Kingsnake (Colour Plate 13)

Size:	to about 100 cm (40 in)
Range:	Montane regions of northern Mexico

Three subspecies of the Mexican kingsnake are commonly available: *L. m. greeri*, Durango mountain kingsnake; *L. m. mexicana*, San Luis Potosi kingsnake; and *L. m. thayeri*, Thayer's kingsnake. All are highly variable in markings, and there is some confusion regarding their taxonomic status. All are tri-coloured kingsnakes, but the bands may be narrow, and the ground colour is grey or greenish.

In captivity, they may all be treated in the same manner as *L. alterna*. Once again, these are montane snakes and it is essential to cool them down in the winter, to 15°C (59°F) or even 12°C (53°F), if they are to produce fertile eggs. Sexual maturity may be achieved within two years.

Availability: All three subspecies of the Mexican kingsnake are produced in fair numbers by breeders and captive-bred hatchlings are readily available.

Breeding data (from literature, R. Applegate, H. Cohen, V. Scheidt)

Time of mating:	March–June
Mating–egg-laying:	24–46 days
Number of eggs:	*greeri*; 3–11 (average of 33 clutches, 5.9) *mexicana*; 9–15 (average of 12 clutches, 12.2) *thayeri*; 5–8 (average of 8 clutches, 6.4)
Incubation period:	54–82 days
Hatch-rate:	Usually high, over 90%, unless the adults are not cooled sufficiently
Size of young:	24–29 cm ($9\frac{1}{2}$–$11\frac{1}{2}$ in)
First food:	Pink mice, lizards

KEY REFERENCES:

Applegate, R. (1987). 'Captive breeding of the Durango Mountain Kingsnake (*Lampropeltis mexicana greeri*) and the Arizona Mountain Kingsnake (*Lampropeltis pyromelana*)'. *Proc. 1987 Symp. Northern Calif. Herp. Soc.* This paper also appears in *Herptile* 12(4).

Tryon, B. W. and Murphy, J. B. (1982). 'Miscellaneous notes on the reproductive biology of reptiles. 5. Thirteen varieties of the genus *Lampropeltis*, species *mexicana*, *triangulum* and *zonata*'. *Transactions of the Kansas Academy of Sciences* 85(2):96–119.

Lampropeltis pyromelana   Arizona Mountain Kingsnake, Sonoran Mountain Kingsnake (Colour Plate 14)

Size:	to about 100 cm (40 in)
Range:	mountain ranges in south-western United States and adjacent northern Mexico

All three subspecies of this snake (*infralabialis*, *pyromelana* and *woodini*) are typical tri-coloured kingsnakes; bands of black, red and white ring the body, the black bands sometimes being wedge-shaped, especially towards the tail, where they may meet along the mid-line of the snake, splitting the red areas. The snout is invariably white. The subspecies are difficult to tell apart, and are often identified on the basis of their origin.

This species requires a medium-sized cage with a hide-box or drawer. Although most specimens feed readily on mice, some are finicky and will only take food if it is placed in their hide-box. In my experience, they frequently cease feeding at the end of the summer, regardless of temperature, etc. and must be cooled down at this time. Because of this, it is important to feed them well when they *are* feeding, otherwise they grow very slowly, and are poor breeders. This is a montane species which must be cooled down, to at least 15°C (59°F) preferably 12°C (53°F) during winter, if breeding is to be attempted. Breeding size can be achieved within two years, although some specimens take three or four years.

Availability: Subspecies *pyromelana* and *woodini* are bred in fairly large numbers and are usually available. *Infralabialis* is less frequently offered.

Breeding data (from literature, R. Applegate, H. Cohen, V. Scheidt)

Time of mating:	March–April
Mating to egg-laying:	32–59 days
Number of eggs:	1–9 (average of 20 clutches, 5.9)
Incubation period:	58–68 days
Size of hatchlings:	23–27 cm (9–10½ in)
First food:	Pink mice, lizards

Key references: *see* previous species.

Lampropeltis ruthveni   Queretaro Kingsnake

Size:	to around 100 cm (40 in)
Range:	northern Mexico

The Queretaro kingsnake is similar in appearance to *L. zonata*. Its care is also similar to that species.

Availability: This species has only been bred during the last few years, but will undoubtedly become more widely available.

Breeding data (from R. Applegate)

Time of mating:	April–June
mating–egg-laying:	32–46 days

Number of eggs: 6–10 (average of 7 clutches, 8.2)
Incubation period: 57–66 days
Hatch-rate: Over 90%
Size of young: 26–29 cm ($10\frac{1}{2}$–$11\frac{1}{2}$ in)
First food: Pink mice

Lampropeltis triangulum   Milk Snake

Size: 80–150 cm (32–60 in), depending on subspecies
Range: Most of North and Central America, into northern South America

Many subspecies of this wide-ranging and highly variable snake are recognised. The nominate subspecies, *L. t. triangulum*, is a grey snake with saddles of rich brown edged in black (i.e. not tri-coloured) but the species becomes progressively more colourful towards the south of its range. Not all forms are bred in captivity, but the most distinctive are briefly described below.

Care of milk snakes is fairly straightforward: a medium-sized cage with a hide-box, and a diet of mice. However, preferred temperatures may be expected to vary somewhat considering the large north-south range of this species. Central American forms require temperatures around 25–30°C (77–86°F), those from northern North America somewhat less, although in a set-up providing a thermal gradient, as described in Chapter 3, all subspecies can be given similar treatment. Relative popularity of the subspecies depends not only on colour but also on size. Several of the North American forms are small and therefore produce proportionately small hatchlings: these will rarely, if ever, take pink mice straight away and can be troublesome to rear. The most frequently seen subspecies are as follows:

L. t. annulata   Mexican Milk Snake

This subspecies grows to around 75 cm (30 in). It is boldly ringed, the pale bands often being yellow or orange, and the snout is nearly always black. Adults should be cooled to 12–15°C (53–59°F) during the winter.

Availability: One of the most frequently bred subspecies, and therefore freely available.

Breeding data (from literature, R. Applegate, H. Cohen, V. Scheidt)

Time of mating: March–May
Mating–egg-laying: 28–63 days (second clutches are frequently produced, in late summer)

Number of eggs: 2–12 (average of 36 clutches, 7.4)
Incubation period: 54–73 days
Hatch-rate: High, usually over 90%
Size of hatchlings: 24–26 cm ($9\frac{1}{2}$–$10\frac{1}{2}$ in)
First food: Pink mice

L. t. campbelli   Pueblan Milk Snake (Colour Plate 15)

Size: to about 100 cm (40 in)
Range: Mexico

A boldly marked tri-coloured milk snake, with wide bands of deep red and rich creamy white. In captivity, this subspecies can be treated exactly as the previous form.

Availability: Although these snakes are being produced in fair numbers by certain breeders they are not as freely available as several other subspecies.

Breeding data (from R. Applegate)

Time of mating: March–May
Mating–egg-laying: 26–54 days (second clutches are frequently produced)
Number of eggs: 6–12 (average of 23 clutches, 7.6)
Incubation period: 63–74 days, at 28°C (82°F)
Hatch-rate: Varies, but frequently 100%
Size of young: 25–26 cm (10–$10\frac{1}{2}$ in)
First food: Pink mice

L. t. hondurensis   Honduran Milk Snake (Colour Plate 16)

Size: to about 250 cm (100 in)
Range: Central America

A large and spectacular subspecies. The red bands are broad and, in good examples, of a deep carmine-red. Unfortunately, many of the original stock showed a tendency to become darker with age due to the suffusion of black pigment on the red scales. Selective breeding has eliminated this tendency in good strains. The so-called 'tangerine' phase differs from the normal animals in that the white rings are replaced with orange or red, sometimes almost matching in colour the broad red bands. However, normal and tangerine animals represent extremes in a continuum of colour variation, and intermediate forms are frequently seen.

Availability: A very popular subspecies with breeders and usually freely available in both colour phases.

Breeding data (from literature, R. Applegate, H. Cohen, V. Scheidt)

Time of mating:	April–June
Mating–egg-laying:	22–49 days
Number of eggs:	2–10 (average of 19 clutches, 6.5)
Incubation period:	57–72 days, typically 66 days at 28°C (82°F)
Hatch-rate:	Usually over 90%, frequently 100%
Size of hatchlings:	35–39 cm (14–15 in)
First food:	Pink mice

KEY REFERENCE:

Howard, C. J. (1985). 'Husbandry and breeding of the Honduran milk snake, *Lampropeltis triangulum hondurensis* at Twycross Zoo'. *Herptile* 10(3):81–84.

L. t. nelsoni   Nelson's Milk Snake

Size: to about 100 cm (40 in)
Range: Mexico

In appearance, this subspecies is similar to *L. t. sinaloae*, differing only in minor details. The number of annuli is usually smaller, often around fifteen.

Availability: Nelson's milk snake is not as frequently bred as the following subspecies. However, it is listed by several breeders and should not be too difficult to obtain.

Breeding data (from R. Applegate)

Time of mating:	April–May
Mating–egg-laying:	48–64 days
Number of eggs:	3–10 (average of 15 clutches, 6.0)
Incubation period:	54–65 days
Hatch-rate:	Usually over 80%, frequently 100%
Size of hatchlings:	24–29 cm (9–11 in)
First food:	Pink mice

KEY REFERENCE:

Tryon, B. W. and Hulsey, T. G. (1976). 'Notes on reproduction in captive *Lampropeltis triangulum nelsoni*'. *Herp. Review* 7(4):161–162.

L. t. sinaloae   Sinaloan Milk Snake (Colour Plate 17)

Size: up to 100 cm (40 in)
Range: Mexico

Perhaps the prettiest of all the milk snakes, this subspecies has broad bands of pure red, evenly broken by triads of jet black and white.

Availability: Although probably bred in greater numbers than any of the other subspecies, this snake is highly desirable and offspring are often spoken-for long before they hatch.

Breeding data (from literature, R. Applegate, H. Cohen, V. Scheidt)

Time of mating:	May–June
Mating–egg-laying:	26–49 days (a second clutch may be produced in as little as 44 days after the first)
Number of eggs:	4–16 (average of 41 clutches, 8.9)
Incubation period:	58–76 days
Hatch-rate:	About 90% overall, frequently 100%
Size of hatchlings:	26–30 cm ($10\frac{1}{2}$–$12\frac{1}{2}$ in)
First food:	Pink mice

KEY REFERENCE:

Nolan, M. (1981). 'Notes on the care and captive breeding of the Sinaloan milk snake (*Lampropeltis triangulum sinaloae*)'. *Bull. Brit. Herp. Soc.* 4:40–44.

OTHER SUBSPECIES:

A number of other subspecies are bred in captivity on an irregular basis, although captive-bred young or wild adults may be available from time to time. These include *L. t. amaura*, the Louisiana milk snake; *L. t. elapsoides*, the scarlet milk snake; *L. t. gentilis*, the Central Plains milk snake; and *L. t. triangulum*, the eastern milk snake. Although several of these are attractive and easily maintained in captivity, they suffer from the drawback of producing very small hatchlings and are therefore unsuitable for captive breeding except for the specialist. In addition, *L. t. polyzona*, and *L. t. arcifera*, the Jalisco milk snake, are recent additions to several breeding stocks; these are larger subspecies, with colourful hatchlings which unfortunately become duller with age – selective breeding may eventually improve them.

KEY REFERENCES:

Tryon, B. W. and Murphy, J. B. (1982). 'Miscellaneous notes on the reproductive biology of reptiles. 5. Thirteen varieties of the genus *Lampropeltis*, species *mexicana*, *triangulum* and *zonata*'. *Transactions of the Kansas Academy of Sciences*, 85(2):96–119.

Blatchford, D. (1985). 'The Jalisco milk snake (*Lampropeltis triangulum arcifera*)'. *Herptile* 10(3):85–89.

Lampropeltis zonata   Californian Mountain Kingsnake (Colour Plate 18)

Size: to 100 cm (40 in)
Range: mountain ranges of California, Oregon and Baja California

A beautiful tri-coloured snake with 23–56 triads of black-white-black between each broad red band. Towards the tail the amount of red is reduced, and occasional specimens are found with no red whatsoever. The snout is black. At least six subspecies are recognised, but differences between them are slight: accurate identification depends largely on knowing the origin of the specimen in question. As far as is known, they do not differ significantly in their requirements or breeding habits and are therefore dealt with together.

This montane species, like its Sonoran counterpart, is secretive, living among rock-piles and in crevices. It therefore requires plenty of cover in its cage, which may be of the drawer-type. In the wild state it probably eats mainly lizards and occasional specimens are reluctant to take mice unless they are first rubbed with a lizard in order to transfer some of its smell. Hatchlings may require a diet of small lizards, e.g. skinks, before accepting pink mice. This species spends several months in hibernation; captive breeding is only successful if the adults are cooled down to 10–13°C (50–55°F) for two to three months in the winter.

Availability: At the time of writing, this species is totally protected in California and neither wild or captive-bred animals are permitted to be sold in the state. However, breeders in other parts of the world produce small numbers of offspring which are offered from time to time.

Breeding data (from literature)

Time of mating:	March–April
Mating–egg-laying:	34–56 days
Number of eggs:	3–8 (average of 6 clutches, 4.3)
Incubation period:	48–67 days
Hatch-rate:	High, usually over 90%
Size of hatchlings:	23–27 cm (9–10$\frac{1}{2}$ in)
First food:	Lizards, rarely pink mice unless force-fed

KEY REFERENCES:

Coote, J. (1984). 'Second generation captive breeding of the Californian mountain kingsnake (*Lampropeltis zonata multicincta*)'. *IHS Symposium Proceedings 1984*.

Tryon, B. W. and Murphy, J. B. (1982). 'Miscellaneous notes on the reproductive biology of reptiles. 5. Thirteen varieties of the genus *Lampropeltis*, species *mexicana*, *triangulum* and *zonata*'. *Transactions of the Kansas Academy of Sciences*, 85(2):96–119.

CHAPTER 9

Genus *Elaphe* – Ratsnakes

The ratsnakes comprise a widespread genus of medium-sized snakes which include several of the most popular and suitable snakes for captive maintenance and breeding, one of which, the corn snake, *Elaphe guttata*, is bred in greater numbers by far than any other species of snake. The genus as a whole is widespread in distribution, but it is the seven North American species which are the most frequently kept in captivity, although several of the European and Asian species also have their following. There is ample scope for the specialist to build up a collection consisting entirely of snakes of this genus, since many of the species exist in distinct colour phases or subspecies, and several have produced colour mutations which are perpetuated by breeders.

Most ratsnakes are active and several species habitually climb. Their cages should be designed in such a way as to allow for this and it may be useful to include a stout branch for some of them. Other than this, their care is straightforward and they are among the easiest species to keep and breed. With the possible exception of some of the lesser-known Asian species, all eat rodents, ranging in size from newborn mice to rats. Most specimens feed well, even as hatchlings, and rearing them presents few problems.

A characteristic which is shared by several members of the genus is that of widely differing juvenile and adult coloration: hatchlings of most species are blotched or banded, but these markings often fade to produce a uniform adult coloration, or one in which the markings consist of longitudinal stripes.

Elaphe bairdi   Baird's Ratsnake (Plate 18)

    Size: to about 100 cm (40 in)
    Range: Southern Texas (Big Bend and Trans-Pecos regions) and
                adjacent areas of Northern Mexico.

Baird's ratsnake, which was formerly thought to be a subspecies of *Elaphe obsoleta* (*see* page XX), is actually fairly distinctive. Juveniles are grey, with about 50 crossbars of darker grey or brown. Smaller blotches of the same colour are present on the flanks. The adults are totally different. The ground colour is still basically grey, bit this is suffused with gold on the head and front part of the body. In addition, four dusky stripes, two on the dorsum and one on each flank, run from the neck region to the tail. Examples from Mexico are considered to be more colourful than those from Texas, the head region often being slate-blue, and the lower parts of the body golden-orange.

Baird's ratsnakes are not common, and their habitat is remote and difficult to collect in. Therefore they are one of the least known of the North American ratsnakes. They appear, nevertheless, to adapt very well to captivity, being docile and undemanding as to food, etc. A temperature of 25–30°C (77–86°F) is required during the summer, and should be cooled to about 15°C (59°F) in winter to ensure successful breeding. The hatchlings take pink mice readily and growth can be rapid, sexual maturity being possible within two years.

Availability: Despite its scarcity in the wild, this species is now produced in fairly large numbers by several snake-breeders. As a consequence, prices have come down and the species is readily available, although in limited numbers.

18. Baird's Ratsnake, *Elaphe bairdi*, a species which is rare in the wild, but bred in fair numbers in captivity. As the snake grows, the crossbars will gradually fade, and two indistinct longitudinal stripes will replace them.

Breeding data (from literature, H. Cohen, V. Scheidt)

Time of mating:	April–May
Mating–egg-laying:	Not known
Number of eggs:	3–14 (average of 12 clutches, 9.1)
Incubation period:	62–71 days
Hatch-rate:	Invariably high, usually 100%
Size of hatchlings:	35–40 cm (14–16 in)
First food:	Pink mice taken without problems

Elaphe climacophora   Japanese Ratsnake

Limited data is available, from literature and H. Cohen. Of 6 recorded clutches, ranging from 5–10 eggs (average 7.3), 3 were infertile, the others hatching at the rates of 77%, 100% and 112.5% (the latter including an egg which produced twins). The incubation period was 46–53 days at 28°C (82°F).

Elaphe dione   Dione's Ratsnake

This Asian ratsnake is occasionally imported, and apparently adapts well to captivity. It grows to 100 cm (40 in), and is pale brown or grey with darker brown blotches. It eats mice and requires a temperature of about 25°C (77°F) during the summer. Breeding has been achieved but no data is available; apparently, the adults must be cooled down to at least 15°C (59°F) during the winter.

Elaphe flavirufa

Very little information is available on this Central American species. Data from literature and V. Scheidt give clutch sizes of 4 and 8 eggs, which hatched in 81–90 days.

Elaphe guttata   Corn Snake, Red Ratsnake (Colour Plate 19)

Size:	to 120 cm (40 in)
Range:	South-eastern North America, into eastern Mexico

A well-known and beautiful snake, of which two, possibly three, subspecies are recognised. These are dealt with separately.

The nominate form, *Elaphe guttata guttata*, is a grey or tan snake with a series of large, black-edged, red saddles along its back. The first dorsal marking extends forward onto the head where it forms a point, while another red stripe crosses the snout and passes through each eye. The underside is chequered in black and white, often with some flecks of red or orange. There is much variation between specimens, those coming from the Okeetee region of South Carolina being especially prized for their intense colour and well-defined belly markings. Specimens from southern Florida have very little black around the saddles or on the underside. These are sometimes given subspecific status, as *E. g. rosacea*, the rosy ratsnake. In addition, many colour mutations are available (*see* below).

The corn snake has no special requirements in captivity. Any of the cages described in Chapter 2 would be suitable, and a temperature of around 25°C (77°F) is called for. Most corn snakes will eat mice of appropriate size throughout their lives, although hatchlings are sometimes too small to take pinkies at first. Growth is rapid and sexual maturity is reached within two years (in fact, females have been known to breed at about eleven months of age, but this is not really a practical proposition since the resulting offspring are small and the female's growth is interrupted).

Availability: Corn snakes are the most easily obtained of all snakes, many thousands being bred annually. In addition to the normal (wild) animals, a number of distinct colour mutants are offered. These include the following:

Amelanistic:	specimens in which the black pigment is absent.
Anerythristic:	specimens in which the red pigment is absent.
'Snow' corns:	specimens in which both of the above conditions are combined, i.e. the snakes are white.
blood-red:	A strain developed in Florida in which the complete animal is suffused with a deep red pigment.

The plains ratsnake, *Elaphe guttata emoryi*, is similar in appearance to the corn snake except that the blotches are rich brown instead of red. Also, the general impression is of a much more robust appearance. Care and breeding are as for the corn snake, and, if anything, this subspecies is even less demanding.

In addition, corn snakes have been hybridised with several other species of snakes, for instance black ratsnakes, *Elaphe obsoleta*, and gopher snakes, *Pituophis melanoleucus*, to produce a wide assortment of artificial strains, the desirability of which is questionable (for discussion, *see* Chapter 6).

Breeding data (from literature, R. Allen, H. Cohen, V. Scheidt)

Time of mating: March–June
Mating–egg-laying: 27–47 days (second clutches are frequent, produced in late summer)
Number of eggs: 8–26 (average of 40 clutches, 15.7)
Incubation period: 55–73 days, typically 62 days at 28°C (82°F)
Hatch-rate: About 80% overall, but often 100%
Size of hatchlings: Variable, 20–28 cm (8–11 in). Some strains seem to produce smaller than average eggs and young. Although the reason for this is not clear, breeding from young females is best avoided
First food: Usually pinkies, but some hatchlings are so small that they must be force-fed, e.g. with a pinkie-pump (*see* Chapter 5)

Elaphe longissima   Aesculapian Snake

Size: to around 150 cm (60 in)
Range: Central and South-eastern Europe

The Aesculapian snake is a slender olive-brown species, often with small white flecks among its scales. Juveniles are patterned with a more or less random arrangement of small dark spots.

Although this species is rarely kept in captivity, it usually adapts well. It feeds on small rodents, and should be given a temperature of about 22–25°C (71–77°F) during the summer, with a drop to 15°C (59°F) or less in the winter.

There is very little information on breeding. Clutches of 6, 8 and 11 eggs, laid June–July, have been recorded. These take 47–61 days to hatch and the young measure 25–28 cm (10–11 in). Despite their slenderness, they apparently take newborn mice readily.

Elaphe moellendorffi   Red-headed Ratsnake

The best examples of this Asian ratsnake are somewhat similar in appearance and coloration to the corn snake, but are much larger, to 200 cm (80 in). Others have brownish saddles, only the head and front portion of the body being reddish.

Although the species has a reputation as a poor captive, this probably stems from the pathetic condition in which most Asian snakes arrive at their destination. Examples which survive the first few months of captivity usually settle down well, eating mice, and thriving at a temperature of about 20°C (68°F). Breeding has been achieved, but only limited data is available: a clutch of 6 eggs began to hatch after 80 days.

Elaphe obsoleta American Ratsnake

This is the most wide-ranging and variable of all of the North American *Elaphe* species, occurring over the whole eastern half of the United States, and just into Canada. Several of the subspecies are so distinct that they will be dealt with separately:

Elaphe o. obsoleta Black Ratsnake (Colour Plate 20)

Size: to around 180 cm (72 in), exceptionally much bigger
Range: this subspecies accounts for the whole of the northern part of the range of the species

The adult black ratsnake, in its pure form, is solid black, but some individuals may retain traces of the juvenile pattern, which consists of a number of large dark grey saddles on a pale grey ground. As the snake grows, the areas between the blotches darken in colour.

This species is a robust snake, well suited to captivity, although wild-caught specimens can be nervous and aggressive at first. It is a powerful constrictor, feeding on mice and small rats, and usually presents few problems. Adults from which it is hoped to breed should be cooled down to 15°C (59°F) at least during the winter, otherwise temperatures of around 25°C (77°F) are indicated. Growth is rapid and sexual maturity can be attained within two years, by which time the snakes should measure about 100 cm (40 in). This species climbs well and may be given a branch to enable it to do so.

Availability: Although black ratsnakes are bred in large numbers, it is normally only the amelanistic colour mutation which receives attention. This is a great shame as good, i.e. solid black, specimens are very handsome snakes.

Breeding data (from literature and R. Applegate)

Time of mating:	March–May
Mating–egg-laying:	27–28 days (second clutches may be produced in August)
Number of eggs:	6–14 (average of 10 clutches, 9.7)
Incubation period:	47–84 days, typically 59 days at 28°C (82°F)
Hatch-rate:	About 90% overall. An egg containing two snakes has been reported

Size of hatchlings: 29–34 cm ($11\frac{1}{2}$–$13\frac{1}{2}$ in)
First food: Pink mice

Note. An interesting record of natural breeding of this snake comes from Jeremy Sloan of Marshall, Montana. A clutch of 11 eggs was found in a rotting tree-stump. These were allowed to develop at ambient temperature and in part of the substrate in which they were found. All hatched on August 23–25, with the young measuring approximately 28 cm (11 in). This compares well with data from captive breedings.

Elaphe o. quadrivittata   Yellow Ratsnake

Size: to 180 cm (72 in)
Range: the Carolinas and Florida

Although the yellow ratsnake begins life with much the same markings as the previous subspecies, its subsequent development is completely different. In this form, the dorsal saddles gradually fade, while the ground colour becomes yellowish. As this is occurring, four dark longitudinal stripes gradually appear along the length of the snake until, at maturity, these are the only markings on a plain yellow ground. The shade of yellow varies somewhat, the best examples being clear golden-yellow.

This is possibly the most arboreal of all the subspecies. It may be treated in much the same way as the previous one, but, in keeping with its distribution, it does not need to be cooled to such an extent in the winter, 20°C (68°F) probably being sufficient. The snake will double-clutch every year, especially if warmed up early in the season. An example of the breeding potential of this snake is provided by the records of Henry Cohen of New York: a female produced 2 clutches each year from 1977 to 1986, totalling 373 eggs in 20 clutches.

Availability: This subspecies is not bred in large numbers, nor are there any colour mutations available. Wild-caught examples are commonly offered, but are rarely as colourful or tractable as captive-bred animals.

Breeding data (from literature and H. Cohen)

Time of mating: March–June
Mating to egg-laying: 45–53 days
Number of eggs: 10–23 (average of 23 clutches, 17.6)
Incubation period: 50–90 days
Hatch-rate: About 80% overall, slightly lower for second clutches
Size of hatchlings: 28–31 cm (11–$12\frac{1}{2}$ in)
First food: Pink mice

Elaphe o. rossalleni   Everglades Ratsnake

   Size: to about 180 cm (72 in)
   Range: Southern Florida

The Everglades ratsnake is an orange version of the previous subspecies and is regarded by many authorities as merely a colour variation. Nevertheless, good examples are among the most beautiful of the ratsnakes, being a bright golden-orange with contrasting longitudinal stripes. Several strains have been selectively bred for good colour, but since the juveniles are identical to all other subspecies, it is essential to see the parents in order to assess their potential.

   Care of this subspecies is identical to that of the previous one.

   Availability: Although several breeders produce this subspecies, supplies are limited. Wild-caught adults are frequently available but are almost always inferior in all respects to captive-bred animals.

Breeding data (from literature and R. Allen)

Time of mating:	May–July
Mating–egg-laying:	33–58 days
Number of eggs:	5–16 (average of 8 clutches, 11)
Incubation period:	45–76 days, typically 68–72 days at 28°C (82°F)
Hatch-rate:	60% overall, but often 100%
Size of hatchlings:	23–30 cm (9–12 in)
First food:	Pink mice

Elaphe o. spiloides   Grey Ratsnake (Plate 19)

   Size: to 180 cm (72 in)
   Range: Mississippi, Alabama and parts of adjacent states

The grey ratsnake is the one subspecies of *obsoleta* in which the juvenile markings are retained throughout life. Unfortunately, the range of this attractive form meets those of several other subspecies and many specimens are intergrades.

   Care of this subspecies as for the black ratsnake. Adults should be cooled to 15°C (59°F) or less before breeding.

   Availability: This subspecies is only bred in small numbers. Wild-caught examples are sometimes available, but the variability in their markings should be considered if buying unseen.

Breeding data (from literature and R. Allen)

Time of mating: March–April
mating–egg-laying: About 37 days
Number of eggs: 9–16 (average of 4 clutches, 12.75)
Incubation period: 52–70 days
Hatch-rate: 64% overall
Size of hatchlings: 35–40 cm (14–16 in)
First food: Pink mice

OTHER SUBSPECIES:

Elaphe o. lindheimeri, the Texas ratsnake, and *E. o. williamsi*, the Gulf hammock ratsnake, are the two remaining subspecies of this snake, but are not often kept. Their care is identical to that of the yellow ratsnake.

Elaphe quatuorlineata　Four-lined Snake (Plate 20)

Size: to about 150 cm (60 in), occasionally larger
Range: Italy, South-eastern Europe

The four-lined snake is the largest of the European ratsnakes, and one of the largest in the genus. It is heavily built, with a broad head. The juveniles are grey with dark, almost black, blotches down the back. These blotches fade as the snake grows and most adults are greyish with four dark longitudinal lines, and a dark line through each eye, but specimens from eastern parts of the range retain traces of the juvenile pattern (subspecies *sauromates*).

Four-lined snakes require a large cage, preferably with an opportunity to climb. Their food consists of mice, even the hatchlings being large enough to tackle well-grown pinkies. A temperature of 25°C (77°F) is sufficient and this species almost certainly needs to be cooled down to 10–15°C (50–59°F) in the winter if breeding is to occur. In my experience, the species is sometimes liable to cease feeding for no apparent reason: hopefully, captive-bred stock will be better adapted.

Availability: This species is protected throughout its range. However, there must be a good reservoir of specimens in private hands and these should form the basis of a supply of captive-bred hatchlings in the future.

There is very little detailed information available on breeding. Two clutches of 6 eggs are recorded, both laid in August. The incubation period was 24—34 days at 26°C (78°F) and the hatchlings measured over 30 cm (12 in).

19. A young Grey Ratsnake, *Elaphe obsoleta spiloides*, the only subspecies in which the juvenile markings do not change thoughout life.

20. Four-lined Snake, *Elaphe quatuorlineata*, a large European species which has not received very much attention from snake-keepers.

Elaphe rufodorsata

Very little information is available on this small Asian species, which is unusual in the genus in eating only frogs. Three clutches of 7 eggs are recorded, all resulting from wild matings. The hatchlings measured 16–19 cm ($6\frac{1}{2}$–$7\frac{1}{2}$ in) in length and ate small frogs.

Elaphe scalaris   Ladder Snake (Colour Plate 21)

    Size: to about 150 cm (60 in)
    Range: South-west Europe

The ladder snake is a brown snake with a pair of dark stripes running down the length of its back. Juveniles are much paler, almost white, with numerous crossbars linking the dorsal stripes, producing the 'ladder' pattern. These fade as the ground colour darkens.

This species is easily kept, although wild-caught specimens may be aggressive at first. It eats mice readily, and requires a temperature of about 25°C (77°F). It is rarely bred in captivity, although a clutch of 4 is recorded from a captive mating.

Elaphe schrenki   Russian Ratsnake

    Size: to about 150 cm (60 in)
    Range: Central Asia

The Russian ratsnake is a slender species with a ground colour of dark brown, dark grey or black, on which are about 20 narrow crossbands of white or yellow.

It is rarely kept in captivity due to limited availability, but appears to be easy to keep and breed. It requires a temperature of around 25°C (77°F), and appreciates a branch on which to climb. It eats mice of appropriate size at all stages of its life. The adults should be cooled down to 10°C (50°F) during the winter if breeding is to take place.

Breeding data (from literature, H. Cohen, V. Scheidt)

Time of mating:	Jan–August
Mating–egg-laying:	32–43 days
Number of eggs:	9–14 (average of 11 clutches, 11.2)
Incubation period:	32–44 days, typically 36–39 days at 28°C (82°F)
Hatch-rate:	High, usually more than 90%
Size of young:	29–38 cm (11–15 in)
First food:	Pink mice

Elaphe situla   Leopard Snake

Size: to about 75 cm (30 in)
Range: South-eastern Europe

This small species is one of the prettiest in the genus. Two types of pattern are found, one in which the pale grey or cream background is marked with a series of black-edged red saddles along the dorsal mid-line, and another in which the red markings take the form of two longitudinal stripes. Intermediate forms in which the blotches are divided into two parallel rows also occur. The markings on the head are black, with a bold line crossing the snout from eye to eye, another from the eye to the upper jaw and a third running backwards from the eye to the angle of the jaw. Juveniles and adults are identical in markings.

The leopard snake has long had a reputation for being difficult to maintain in captivity. However, this is not always so and, although some animals refuse to feed voluntarily, others are among the most undemanding of all snakes. They require a temperature of 25–30°C (77–86°F) and are content with a small cage. Adults should be cooled down, probably to around 15°C (59°F), for three or four months during the winter.

Availability: This species is protected throughout its range, and the only legal source is captive-bred young, the supply of which is extremely limited.

Breeding data is very sparse. This species lays small clutches of about 4 eggs, which hatch after 60–70 days. The hatchlings measure about 33 cm (13 in) and will accept pink mice as well as small lizards.

Elaphe subocularis   Trans-Pecos Ratsnake (Colour Plate 22)

Size: to 150 cm (60 in)
Range: Trans-Pecos and Big Bend regions of the United States and adjacent areas of Mexico

The Trans-Pecos ratsnake is remarkable for its coloration, being one of the few snakes which are predominantly yellow. It varies in shade from pale creamy yellow to tan, and two colour phases are recognised, representing the extremes of a continuum of variation. The most commonly encountered phase consists of a deep yellow to ochre ground, marked with 27–41 black H-shaped markings. The so-called 'blond' phase is much paler in general colour, and the dorsal markings are also paler, and circular in shape. The head of both types is invariably unmarked yellow or cream, making the large black eyes especially prominent.

This snake is a nocturnal inhabitant of arid and rocky regions, and was formerly thought to be scarce. In fact, it may be the commonest species of snake in parts of its range, but its short activity period and the limited access into the region in which it lives makes it appear rarer than it is. Trans-Pecos ratsnakes are not difficult to keep and breed in captivity. They require medium-sized cages and a temperature of 25–30°C (77–86°F) during the summer. Their diet consists of mice (although they probably eat mainly lizards in the wild state). Adults from which it is hoped to breed should be cooled down to 15–20°C (59–68°F) during the winter. Growth of the hatchlings is rapid, and sexual maturity can be achieved within two years.

Availability: This species is bred in fairly large numbers and there should be little difficulty in obtaining captive-bred young. Blond phase animals are eagerly sought after and command a much higher price (about double that of the normal form).

Breeding data (from literature)

Time of mating:	May–July
Mating–egg-laying:	33–49 days
Number of eggs:	2–9 (average of 20 clutches, 5.4)
Incubation period:	67–103 days, typically 73 days at 28°C (82°F)
Hatch-rate:	Only about 50% overall, but may be 100%
Size of hatchlings:	33–38 cm (13–15 in)
First food:	Pink mice

KEY REFERENCE:

Tryon, B. (1976). 'Second generation captive reproduction and courtship behaviour in the Trans-Pecos ratsnake, *Elaphe subocularis*'. *Herp. Review* 7(4):156–157.

Elaphe taeniura

Very little information is available on this Asian ratsnake. Matings have been reported for December and February, with clutches of 7–11 taking about 80 days to hatch.

Elaphe triaspis   Green Ratsnake

Size:	to about 120 cm (48 in)
Range:	extreme southern Arizona down into western Mexico

The green ratsnake is a uniform green, grey or olive snake. Many examples are fairly dull in coloration compared to other species of ratsnakes, but green examples are unusual and handsome snakes. The hatchlings are blotched.

Little is known of the natural history of this snake and it is still a rarity in collections. However, it appears to adapt well to captivity, and probably requires similar treatment to the Trans-Pecos ratsnake (*see* above).

A single record of captive breeding is available, from Tom Taylor of Tempe, Arizona, involving the subspecies *E. t. intermedia*. A clutch of 6 eggs were laid in July and these hatched after 56 days. The young measured about 45 cm (18 in). It is likely that this species will become more popular as supplies of captive-bred offspring become available, especially if these are selected for good colour.

Elaphe vulpina   Fox Snake

Size: to about 130 cm (52 in)
Range: North-central region of the United States, Great Lakes region of Canada

The fox snake is a heavy-bodied blotched snake, being light brown with blotches and spots of dark chestnut brown. Adults and young are identical in markings. Two subspecies are recognised, *E. v. vulpina*, the western fox snake, and *E. v. gloydi*, the eastern fox snake. They differ in the number of dorsal blotches, those of *gloydi* being fewer in number, and larger, than those of the nominate form.

Fox snakes are rarely kept in captivity, although they adapt well, and are docile. They need no special treatment, but due to their northern distribution are more tolerant of lower temperatures than many of the other species, and should be kept at about 20–25°C (68–77°F). In my experience, this species ceases to feed in the winter, even if high temperatures are maintained artificially. They should therefore be cooled down to at least 15°C (59°F), preferably lower, until the spring.

I have been unable to trace any records of captive breeding, which is remarkable since this species should not present any difficulties. Clutches obtained from females which were gravid at the time of capture contained from 6–12 eggs (average 8.4).

CHAPTER 10

Genus *Pituophis* – Bull, Gopher and Pine Snakes

The subjects of this chapter consists of the various forms of the species *Pituophis melanoleucus*. These go under the common names of bull snake, gopher snake or pine snake, according to their origin, but all are excellent choices for captivity, providing enough variety for a fairly extensive specialised collection. Furthermore, several of them are relatively common in the wild and therefore reasonably priced.

These snakes are typical 'general purpose' colubrids – medium-sized ground-dwellers which feed on rodents, birds, etc. All are North American in distribution, collectively ranging over almost the entire United States, north into Canada and south into Mexico. Although they occupy a range of habitats, all have similar requirements. These consist of a medium-sized cage with a hide-box or a drawer, a diet of mice and a temperature of 25–30°C (77–86°F) during the summer. Adults should be cooled to about 15°C (59°F) during the winter if it is hoped to breed from them. The hatchlings are large and robust, and rearing them rarely presents any difficulties. They grow rapidly and will mature within two years. Breeding size is about 120 cm (48 in), but adults of some subspecies may eventually reach over 250 cm (100 in), making this one of the largest of the North American serpents. A number of the subspecies have produced mutations, usually consisting of albinos, and some of these are very attractive. The supply of captive-bred offspring is good in the case of the most popular subspecies, although several of the lesser-known ones are bred in limited numbers.

The subspecies are distinctive enough to warrant separate treatment, although breeding data appear to be fairly constant and is therefore pooled.

Breeding data (from literature, R. Applegate, H. Cohen, M. W. Hammock, J. Muir)

Time of mating:	April–May
Mating–egg-laying:	37–67 days

Number of eggs:	3–15 (average of 47 clutches, 6.7)*
Incubation period:	52–72 days, typically 59 days at 28°C (82°F)
Hatch-rate:	Over 75% overall, often 100%
Size of hatchlings:	27–54 cm (10½–21 in), depending on sub-species
First food:	Pink mice taken without difficulty

*the largest clutches are recorded for *P. m. sayi*, other subspecies ranging from 3–10 eggs per clutch, and averaging slightly less than 6.7.

KEY REFERENCES:

Hammock, M. W. 'Reproduction and breeding behaviour in captive black pine snakes'. *Bull. Chi. Herp. Soc.* 19(4):125–130.

Reichling, S. (1982). 'Reproduction in captive black pine snakes, *Pituophis melanoleucus lodingi*'. *Herp. Review* 13(2):41.

THE SUBSPECIES ARE AS FOLLOWS:

P. m. annectans   San Diego Gopher Snake

A cream, yellow or tan snake with bold brown dorsal blotches, those towards the front of the body being almost black.

The San Diego gopher snake is one of the commonest subspecies, but is rarely bred in captivity except in its albino form. These colour mutants are marked in a way that is the reverse of the normal type, the areas which should be dark being almost pure white, but the ground colour being orange or yellow. Strains vary in their exact coloration and several have been given names in order to identify them.

P. m. affinis   Sonoran Gopher Snake (Colour Plate 23)

This is one of the prettiest of the western subspecies, the ground colour usually being a clear yellow-tan and the body blotches rust coloured. This desert gopher snake is rarely bred in captivity, although wild-caught animals are sometimes available. An albino strain is listed by some breeders.

P. m. catenifer   Pacific Gopher Snake

Darker in coloration than the preceding two species, but of basically the same pattern. The ground colour tends towards grey and the dorsal blotches are not so strongly contrasted. Certain naturally occurring populations of Pacific gopher snakes contain a proportion of striped rather than blotched individuals, the ground colour being the same as in

125

normal specimens, with darker stripes. Normal specimens of this subspecies are rarely bred in captivity, but the striped variety and an albino are often listed, and these two types have also been combined to produce an attractive striped albino.

P. m. deserticola   Great Basin Gopher Snake

This subspecies is similar to the Sonoran gopher snake but the dorsal blotches are deeper brown and more extensive, often connecting with the smaller ones on the flanks. It is rarely bred in captivity.

P. m. lodingi   Black Pine Snake

Immaculate black or dark brown, this is one of the most striking and popular subspecies.

Black pine snakes are not common in the wild and captive-bred young command a higher price than most of the other subspecies. However, there is a fairly good supply of them.

P. m. melanoleucus   Northern Pine Snake (Colour Plate 24)

The northern pine snake is possibly the most handsome of the clan. The ground colour is almost white and the black or dark brown dorsal blotches are large and well defined. This subspecies suffers from being more aggressive than the others, hissing and striking at the least provocation. However, it usually strikes with the mouth closed and need not be regarded as a difficult snake to deal with. Despite its attractive appearance, the subspecies is bred in only small numbers.

P. m. mugitus   Florida Pine Snake (Plate 21)

Though basically similar to the previous subspecies, the markings of this form are less well defined. The ground colour is darker, buff or pale brown, while the dorsal blotches are brown, becoming darker towards the tail. The subspecies is rarely bred.

P. m. sayi   Bull Snake

The bull snake is the largest and most impressive of the subspecies. The ground colour is usually yellow but may be tan or orange, while the dorsal blotches are rich chestnut brown or russet, those nearest the head and the tail being darkest. Wild-caught bull snakes can be aggressive and intimidating snakes, but they normally tame down well. Captive-bred

21. Florida Pine Snake, *Pituophis melanoleucus mugitus*, a naturally occurring form in which the dark markings are lacking and the snake is pale fawn all over.

hatchlings soon lose their initial nervousness. The subspecies is not bred in large numbers.

Other subspecies of gopher snake are recognised, including *P. m. ruthveni*, the Louisiana gopher snake, and *P. m. vertebralis*, the Cape gopher snake (from Baja California). In addition, another full species, *Pituophis deppei*, occurs in Mexico. Although I can find no reports of captive breeding relating to any of these snakes, they are all listed occasionally and are undoubtedly worthwhile additions to a collection. Their basic care is identical to that of the species listed above.

CHAPTER 11

Miscellaneous Colubrid Snakes

A large number of snakes belonging to the family Colubridae appear on dealers' lists, and it is not possible to deal with all of them. The following list of species has been selected as representing a fair cross-section of those which the snake-keeper is likely to come across, as well as those species which are regularly bred. Since the family contains a huge diversity of types, it is not possible to give general instructions for their care, but the information given in Chapters 1–6 should provide adequate guide-lines for the majority of species. In general, snakes from South-east Asia should be avoided by beginners since they are notoriously prone to parasites and stress-related diseases due to the atrocious conditions under which they are held and transported prior to sale. In addition, the natural history of many of these species is poorly known and they often have specialised dietary requirements.

On the other hand, there are undoubtedly species among them which have great potential as captives, and there is a great deal of scope for the adventurous enthusiast to experiment. This also applies to those North American, European and African species which, though rarely available, crop up on price lists from time to time, or may be collected.

Arizona elegans   Glossy Snake (Plate 22)

   Size: to 120 cm (48 in)
   Range: North America

The glossy snake is a slender, smooth-scaled species with a pointed snout. It is light brown to tan, with irregular crossbands of darker brown or olive.

   In captivity it requires no special treatment, and will thrive in a medium-sized cage with a water bowl and hide-box. A temperature of 25–30°C (77–86°F) should be maintained during the summer, and mice

1.   Dumeril's Ground Boa, *Acrantophis dumerili*, a rare species from Madagascar, which is now bred in fair numbers.

2.   Common Boa, *Boa constrictor*, one of the most popular snakes. This example is the dwarf form from Hog Island, Honduras, which is also paler in colour than typical common boas.

4.   Brazilian Rainbow Boa, *Epicrates cenchria cenchria*, probably the most beautiful subspecies of this South American boa.

3.   Emerald Tree Boa, *Corallus canina*, a superbly marked arboreal species from the forests of South America. Although occasionally bred in captivity, this is not one of the easiest snakes to keep successfully.

5. Egyptian Sand Boa, *Eryx colubrinus colubrinus*, a wild-caught individual in which the black pigment is lacking.

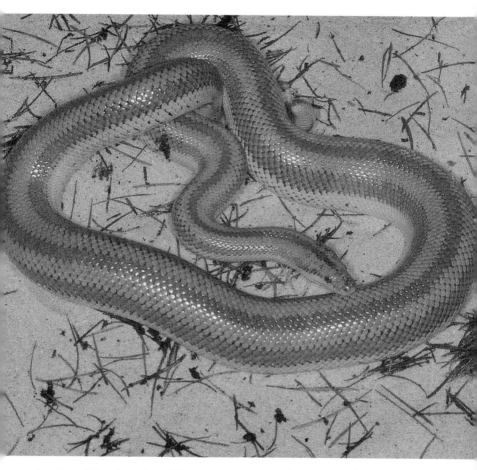

6. Central Baja Rosy Boa, *Lichanura trivirgata myriolepis.*

7. Green Tree Python, *Chondropython viridis*, a firm favourite with most snake-keepers, but totally protected in the wild and difficult to breed.

8. Burmese Python, *Python molurus*. This example is lacking most of its pigment, but is not a complete albino since the eyes are darkly coloured.

9. Californian Kingsnake, *Lampropeltis getulus californiae*, an example of the striped form, which is only found in the San Diego region.

10. Californian Kingsnake, *Lampropeltis getulus californiae*, the black and white banded form from desert areas.

11. Desert Kingsnake, *Lampropeltis getulus splendida*, an example from southern Arizona, in which the markings are white rather than yellow, which is more typical.

12. Grey-banded Kingsnake, *Lampropeltis alterna*, a particularly well-marked example of the 'Blair's phase'.

13. San Luis Potosi Kingsnake, *Lampropeltis mexicana mexicana.*

14. Arizona Mountain Kingsnake, *Lampropeltis pyromelana woodini,* a montane species.

15. A batch of freshly hatched Pueblan Milk Snakes, *Lampropeltis triangulum campbelli*.

16. Honduran Milk Snake, *Lampropeltis triangulum hondurensis*, tangerine phase.

17. Sinaloan Milk Snake, *Lampropeltis triangulum sinaloae*, in the process of laying eggs. Clutches typically consist of about nine eggs.

18. Californian Mountain Kingsnake, *Lampropeltis zonata pulchra*, a beautifully coloured montane species, which often prefers lizards to mice.

19. Corn or Red Ratsnake, *Elaphe guttata*, a species which is bred in huge numbers and in a variety of different colour forms.

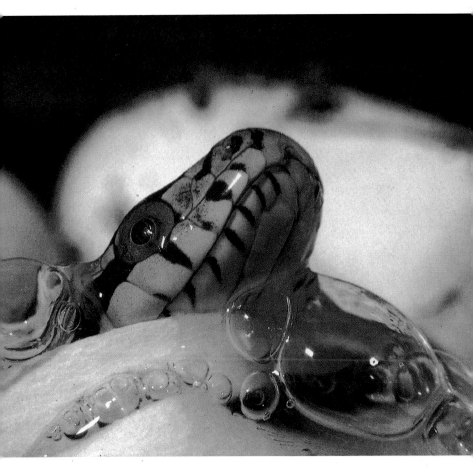

20. Black Ratsnake, *Elaphe obsoleta obsoleta*, hatching from its egg.

21. Ladder Snake, *Elaphe scalaris*, a young specimen – adults lose the crossbars and become darker with age.

22.   Trans-Pecos Ratsnake, *Elaphe subocularis*, a nocturnal species from rocky, arid habitats.

23. Sonoran Gopher Snake, *Pituophis melanoleucus affinis*.

24. Northern Pine Snake, *Pituophis melanoleucus melanoleucus*, possibly the most attractive form of this species.

25. Mangrove Snake, *Boiga dendrophila*, a large back-fanged species from South-East Asia which may be potentially dangerous to humans.

26. Indigo Snake, *Drymarchon corais couperi*, a very popular species, which breeds only irregularly in captivity.

27. Western Hognosed Snake, *Heterodon nasicus*, a species which adapts well to captivity and breeds readily.

28. Longnosed Snake, *Rhinocheilus lecontei*, an attractive desert species from south-western North America which normally eats lizards but can usually be persuaded to take small mice.

29. Chequered Garter Snake, *Thamnophis marcianus*, one of the more
distinct forms of this large genus of North American snakes.

30. San Francisco Garter Snake, *Thamnophis sirtalis tetrataenia*, the most attractive and rarest of the garter snakes. The juvenile illustrated was bred at San Diego Zoo.

31. Eastern Garter Snake, *Thamnophis sirtalis sirtalis*.

32. Gaboon Viper, *Bitis gabonicus*, an enormous viper from the forest regions of Africa.

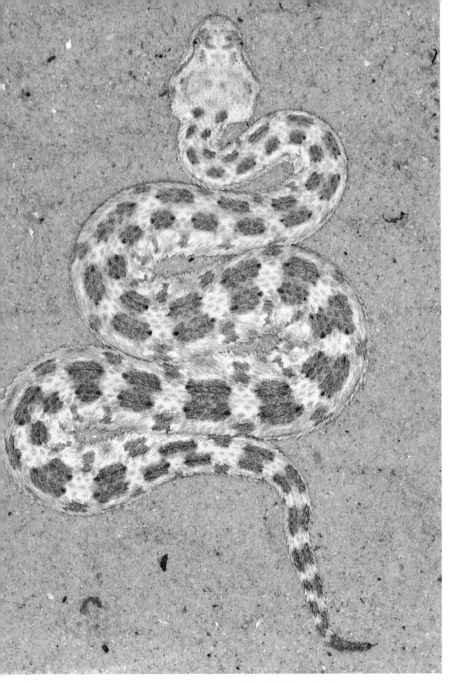

33. Desert Horned Viper, *Cerastes cerastes*, a North African Species.

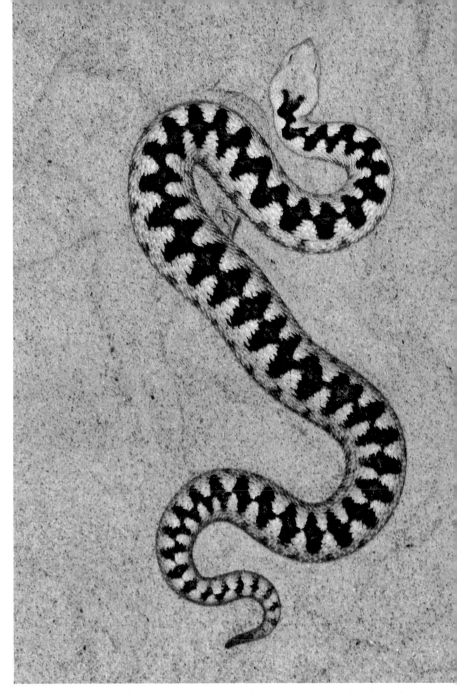

34. Nose-horned Viper, *Vipera ammodytes*, probably the most spectacular of the European venomous snakes.

35. Caucasian Viper, *Vipera kasnakovi*, a rarely seen species from Russia and
northern Turkey, which is docile as well as attractive. It has been bred in
Europe.

36.   Western Diamondback Rattlesnake, *Crotalus atrox*, a large, common and easily cared-for rattler from North America.

37. Sidewinder, *Crotalus cerastes*, a small North American rattler which closely parallels the Desert Horned Viper (Colour Plate 34).

38. Black-tailed Rattlesnake, *Crotalus molossus*, an attractive, though rarely-kept North American species.

39. Pope's Pit Viper, *Trimeresurus popeorum*, one of several very similar
Asian pit vipers which are occasionally kept and bred in captivity.

are readily accepted, even by small individuals. This species does not appear to have been bred in captivity, probably through lack of interest, but it seems likely that a cooling-off period would be required before this occurred.

Boiga dendrophila   Mangrove Snake (Colour Plate 25)

Size: to 200 cm (80 in)
Range: South-east Asia

The mangrove snake is one of the most strikingly marked species, being jet black with narrow, bright yellow crossbands. The upper lips are also bright yellow. It is a slender arboreal species, which kills its prey by means of a venom injected via enlarged rear fangs. THIS SPECIES MAY BE DANGEROUS TO MAN AND REQUIRES A LICENCE UNDER THE DANGEROUS WILD ANIMALS ACT (IN BRITAIN). Wild caught specimens can be aggressive, but long-term captives or captive-bred young are normally quite docile.

It requires a large cage with branches on which to climb. A temperature of 25–30°C (77–86°F) is necessary, although this may be lowered by a few degrees during the winter.

Availability: This species is frequently imported and wild specimens are usually readily obtainable (although their legal status in Britain has

22.   Glossy Snake, *Arizona elegans*, a species from dry regions of North America which thrives in captivity but is rarely kept.

reduced the numbers imported), but their quality varies, as with other Asian reptiles. Captive-bred young may be available from time to time and are always preferable.

Breeding data (from literature and H. Cohen)

Time of mating:	January–June
Mating–egg-laying:	34–51 days (but females have been known to store sperm for considerable periods)
Number of eggs:	4–9 (average of 9 clutches, 5.7)
Incubation period:	93–120 days
Hatch-rate:	Above 80%
Size of hatchlings:	35–37 cm ($13\frac{1}{2}$–$14\frac{1}{2}$ in)
First food:	Hatchlings may require force-feeding with pink mice, although frogs or lizards are usually taken voluntarily

Note: other species of *Boiga* are occasionally available. Their care is basically similar to that of the mangrove snake.

Chionactis occipitalis   Western Shovel-nosed Snake

Size: to about 40 cm (16 in)
Range: desert regions of western North America, in loose sand

A small, burrowing desert snake which spends the greater part of its life beneath the surface. It 'swims' rapidly through fine, wind-blown sand and is rarely seen except when it crosses roads at night. It is pale cream with about 30 black crossbands or rings. On some specimens there are smaller red bands between these black ones.

Care of this interesting little snake is simplicity itself. It requires a small box with about 5 cm (2 in) of fine sand, e.g. silver sand, in which it will spend most of its time. It eats insects, including crickets, mealworms and waxworms, which are merely placed in the box and will be eaten during the night. A small water bowl may be provided, or a small piece of flat stone may be placed at one end of the box and lightly sprayed during the evening, when the snake will drink from the droplets which form on its surface. It requires a temperature of 25–30°C (77–86°F), which is best provided by heat-tape or a heat-pad. Unfortunately, this species does not appear to have been bred in captivity, and so it is not possible to give details; the only forseeable problem would be that of providing a moist area for the eggs to be laid, since they are small and probably susceptible to rapid desiccation.

Genus *Coluber*   Whipsnakes and Racers

This large genus of snakes, which occurs in North America and Europe, and the closely related genus *Masticophis*, from North America, contains an assortment of long, slender, rapidly moving, diurnal snakes. Although they vary in colour and markings, all feature a long, narrow head and large eyes.

In captivity, all these species require very large cages and plenty of cover, for they are nervous and exceedingly active. When first captured, they are inclined to be snappy, and although many of them eventually tame down, others do not. A temperature of 25–30°C (77–86°F) is required during the day, and a natural spectrum fluorescent light may also be beneficial. Most will eat mice, although lizards are probably the natural food, whereas the juveniles are said to eat invertebrates. Although several of these species have undoubtedly laid eggs in captivity, there appear to be no records of captive matings.

Dasypeltis scabra   Egg-eating Snake

Size: to about 60 cm (24 in)
Range: Southern and Central Africa

The egg-eating snake is a slender species with heavily keeled scales (which it may rub together to produce a rustling or hissing sound). Most specimens are brown with darker blotches or chevrons down the back, although there is much variation according to origin. This species is kept more for the interest attached to its feeding habits than for its appearance.

Apart from its food, the species requires nothing by way of special treatment. A small cage is sufficient, kept at a temperature of 25–30°C (77–86°F). This snake is remarkable for its diet, which consists entirely of birds' eggs. These are engulfed whole by the outrageously elastic jaws and worked down into the throat where extensions of the vertebrae saw through the shell, releasing the contents into the oesophagus. The shell is then regurgitated. Adults will take hen's eggs readily, but the young can be problematical to feed. Hatchlings require very small eggs, such as those of canaries or zebra finches. As they grow they will graduate to medium-sized eggs such as those of quail, then of pigeons. With adequate feeding, they will grow quite quickly and reach breeding size in two years.

Availability: This species is not bred or imported in large numbers, but specimens are sometimes available.

Breeding data (from literature)

Time of mating: July

mating to egg-laying: 31 days
Number of eggs: 2–13 (average of 8 clutches, 8.5)
Incubation period: 45–61 days, typically 45 days at 28°C (82°F)
Hatch-rate: Variable
Size of hatchlings: 20 cm (8 in)
First food: See above

Genus *Diadophis*   Ringnecked Snakes

Size: to about 75 cm (30 in), depending on species
Range: North America

Ringnecked snakes are small secretive species, often found beneath rocks, logs, boards, etc. All are superficially similar in appearance: slender dark grey or black snakes with a distinctive red, orange or yellow collar behind the head, and red or yellow undersides. Several species raise the tail if disturbed, displaying the bright ventral coloration.

In captivity these species appear to require a damp environment. A successful method is to keep them in a small box containing an inch or two of peat/sand mixture, with one or two small flat rocks laid on the surface. A small water dish should also be included, and the substrate should be sprayed occasionally, especially beneath the rocks, ensuring that at least part of the cage never dries out completely. Under this arrangement, ringnecked snakes will usually eat earthworms and other soft-bodied invertebrates, and will live for a considerable time. Unfortunately, there are no records of captive breeding, probably due to lack of interest.

Drymarchon corais   Indigo Snake (Colour Plate 26)

Size: to 200 cm (80 in), sometimes much larger
Range: Florida and adjacent parts of adjoining states, southern Texas and Central and South America

Several subspecies of the indigo snake are recognised, but the following notes are based on the most desirable and commonly kept form, the Florida indigo, *D. c. couperi*. This snake is a slender species with large glossy scales. The body is somewhat triangular in cross-section and the colour is a rich black or blue-black, interrupted only by a patch of white or salmon-pink on the chin. Juveniles are mottled in shades of brown (as are the adults of several of the tropical subspecies).

The indigo snake has long been one of the most sought-after species of snakes, due to its beauty and temperament. Unfortunately, habitat destruction has reduced its numbers drastically, resulting in total protection throughout its range. Moreover, this species has presented many problems to the snake-breeder despite continued attempts to find a reliable method of breeding it. Basic care, however, is not difficult. They require a large cage, and a hide-box is essential. Most adults will eat mice, rats and day-old chicks, but young specimens and some adults prefer various other types of prey, including fish, amphibians and snakes. During the winter, a temperature of 25–30°C (77–86°F) is required, but in order to encourage breeding it is essential to allow this to fall to about 15°C (59°F) during the winter. Unlike many North American colubrids, this species mates during the winter, i.e. while the temperature is reduced. At this time the males become aggressive towards each other as well as towards their mates, and animals should be kept separately except when females are introduced to the males for mating, when they should be carefully observed, if possible, in order to prevent serious injuries. Sexual maturity is reached at about 130 cm (52 in), which normally takes three to four years.

The greatest difficulty that has plagued breeders of this snake is that of egg infertility. A common pattern is for pairs to produce good eggs for one or two years and then to produce only infertile clutches. Occasionally, the odd fertile clutch will be produced subsequently, but I can find no records of consistent breeding. Various theories have been put forward to explain this disappointing performance, including lack of vitamin D3, but attempts to rectify it by using light-sources which provide ultra-violet rays and/or using vitamin supplements have met with only limited success. Hopefully, an enterprising group of enthusiasts will eventually get to grips with this problem and supplies of captive-bred indigo snakes will begin to meet the considerable demand.

Breeding data (from literature, H. Cohen and R. Hine)

Time of mating:	November–February, during cool period
Mating–egg-laying:	54–146 days, but females are known to retain sperm
Number of eggs:	4–20 (average of 37 clutches, 9.9)
Incubation period:	70–103 days, typically 85–90 days at 28°C (82°F)
Hatch-rate:	About 60% of all fertile eggs overall, but this figure does not include many clutches which consisted entirely of infertile eggs
Size of hatchlings:	48–60 cm
First food:	Fish, mice, frogs (force-feeding is sometimes necessary)

Erpeton tentaculatum   Fishing Snake

Size: to about 80 cm (32 in)
Range: South-east Asia

This is one of the more bizarre species of snakes. It is totally aquatic and is flattened from top to bottom, being about twice as wide as it is deep. It has a pair of appendages sprouting from its snout, rather like tentacles, small eyes and heavily keeled scales. When handled it appears more rigid than other snakes, and has great difficulty in making any progress on land. It is normally reddish-brown, with two wide longitudinal bands of darker brown running along the back. On the flanks are various spots and blotches of brown, the species being subject to a great deal of variation in markings. Old specimens are frequently covered in algae.

In captivity, this species should be kept in an aquarium, with a temperature of around 25°C (77°F), a substrate of pea-gravel or pebbles, and plenty of aquatic plants, which may consist of bottom-rooting species such as *Vallisneria* or floating species such as Java moss (*Vesicularia dubyana*) and water lettuce (*Pistia*). It often does quite well at first, feeding entirely on living fish, such as goldfish, which it ambushes from among the clumps of plants, but very often becomes infected with fungus which covers its scales, especially in the head region. This eventually spreads and results in the death of the snake. It seems quite likely that some of the cures recommended for treatment of fungus in tropical fish would be effective in overcoming this problem, but so far this does not appear to have been investigated.

I can find no records of captive breeding, and doubt whether this has been achieved. In keeping with its habitat, this species is live-bearing.

Heterodon nasicus   Western Hognosed Snake (Colour Plate 27)

Size: to 60 cm (24 in)
Range: central states of North America, into northern Mexico

Three subspecies of this snake are recognised. All are stout snakes with heavily keeled scales, and the distinctive upturned snout which gives them their common name. The nominate form, *H. n. nasicus*, is pale brown or buff, with highly contrasting markings of darker brown along the back and flanks. In both the other subspecies, *H. n. kennerlyi*, the Mexican hognosed snake, and *H. n. gloydi*, the dusty hognosed snake, the markings are less distinct. They differ from each other in minor scalation details.

Care of the western hognosed snake is simple and this species can be highly recommended. It requires only a small cage equipped with a hide-box, and a diet of mice. A temperature of about 25°C (77°F) is necessary during the summer, and this should be lowered to 15°C (59°F) during the winter if breeding is planned. The hatchlings grow quickly and can attain breeding size by the time they are two years old.

Availability: This species was rarely kept in captivity until a few years ago, when it was found to be easily maintained and bred. Since then, the supply of captive-bred young has steadily improved, although *gloydi* and *kennerlyi* are still in short supply.

Breeding data (from literature, R. Hine and T. Howe)

Time of mating:	March–May
Mating–egg-laying:	Not known
Number of eggs:	9–21 (average of 9 clutches, 11.5)
Incubation period:	45–54 days
Hatch-rate:	Usually 100%
Size of hatchlings:	15 cm (6 in)
First food:	Pink mice

Heterodon platyrhinos   Eastern Hognosed Snake

Size: to 80 cm (30 in)
Range: eastern North America

This species is similar to the previous one but is larger, and has irregular markings. Its general coloration is variable, and may be grey, brown, orange yellowish or black. This snake is remarkable for its defensive behaviour. When first disturbed, most specimens flatten their necks and hiss loudly. If this is not successful they will turn onto their back and feign death. They inhabit dry sandy areas where they burrow into the soil, using their upturned snout.

Care of this species is much as for the previous one, but the eastern hognosed snake suffers as a captive from eating only amphibians, mostly toads of the genus *Bufo*. For this reason it is rarely kept, although breeding has been achieved on several occasions: 10–20 eggs (average 14.3) are laid March to June and a second clutch may be produced in September. They hatch in 51–78 days and the young measure 13–16 cm (5–6½ in). First, and subsequent, food is toads of appropriate sizes.

Hypsiglena torquata   Night Snake (Plate 23)

Size: to 60 cm (24 in)
Range: North and Central America

23. Night Snake, *Hypsiglena torquata*, a small North American colubrid which eats mice as well as lizards in captivity.

The night snake is a small snake, common in a variety of habitats, often found beneath rocks, boards, etc. or active on roads at night. It is brown with darker blotches on the back and sides and a larger dark area just behind the head. It is a back-fanged species but so small as to be totally harmless to humans.

This species is rarely kept in captivity, although it adapts reasonably well. All it requires is a small plastic box or the like, furnished with a place to hide, and a water bowl. Temperature around 25–30°C (77–86°F). It probably eats mainly lizards in the wild, but large specimens will take pink mice. Captive breeding is not recorded, but wild-caught females may lay eggs. Two such clutches, reported by Jean Bradley of National City, California, totalled 5 eggs which took approximately 48 days to hatch. The hatchlings measured 15 cm (6 in) in length and were released; feeding night snakes of this size would undoubtedly be a problem.

Lamprophis fuliginosus   Brown House Snake

   Size: to 110 cm (44 in), occasionally larger
   Range: southern Africa

This species, previously known as *Boaedon fuliginosus*, is one of the commonest African species, and very suitable for captive conditions. It is especially recommended to beginners. It is uniform mid-brown above, with a cream line from the snout, passing back through each eye and fading out just behind the head. The underside is cream or pinkish, with a beautiful pearly sheen.

The brown house snake is among the easiest of snakes to keep and breed. It requires a medium-sized cage with a hide-box, and a temperature of about 25°C (77°F). Its diet is rodents, which it constricts in its powerful coils, and it has a remarkable capacity for taking prey which is seemingly much too large for it. In order to breed this species it is probably essential to cool the adults down to 15–20°C (59–68°F) during the winter, after which it will breed several times during the summer. Hatchlings grow quickly and become sexually mature when they reach 75 cm (30 in), which is easily attainable within two years. An interesting record from Larry Moor of Port Coquitlam, British Columbia, concerns a female which laid 12 eggs, followed by a second clutch on the day the first eggs were hatching, followed by a third clutch as the second was hatching – a very efficient egg-machine!

Availability: Although the brown house snake is not bred in large numbers, demand for it is limited, and so there should be little difficulty in obtaining hatchlings.

Breeding data (from literature and L. Moor)

Time of mating:	February–April (northern hemisphere) October–November (southern hemisphere)
Mating–egg-laying:	Not known
Number of eggs:	2 (from a small female)–15 (average of 15 clutches, 9.7)
Incubation period:	56–83 days, typically 70 days at 28°C (82°F)
Hatch-rate:	Invariably high, over 90%
Size of hatchlings:	18–25 cm (7–10 in)
First food:	Pink mice

Natrix tessellata   Dice Snake

Size:	to about 75 cm (30 in)
Range:	Italy and South-eastern Europe

The dice snake is a semi-aquatic species with a narrow head and keeled scales. It is usually olive-green or brown with many dark spots distributed over the back and flanks. These may be small and indistinct or large and squarish in shape, depending on the locality.

In captivity this species requires a medium-sized cage with a hide-box and a large water dish, kept only half full so that spillage will not occur when the snake submerges itself. A temperature of about 25°C (77°F) is required in the summer, but this may be reduced to 10–15°C (50–59°F) during the winter. This species normally eats fish and amphibians, but can usually be persuaded to accept sliced fish readily. Although I can find no records of captive breeding, this has almost certainly been achieved. Unlike the closely related American *Nerodia* species (which were formerly included in this genus), European 'water' snakes are egg-layers.

Availability: This species was one of the most frequently offered snakes in Europe until recent legislation prevented its collection. Supplies are therefore limited.

Two more species of *Natrix*, *N. natrix*, the grass snake, and *N. maura*, the viperine snake, are found in Europe. Their care is similar to that of the dice snake, although the grass snake is a larger animal which rarely adapts as well to captivity as the other two. Several additional species occur in Asia, but although some of these would undoubtedly make good captives, health problems with imported Asian snakes make it impossible to recommend them.

Genus *Nerodia*   North American Water Snakes (Plate 24)

Size: to about 100 cm (40 in)
Range: eastern North America

The North American 'water' snakes are included in a genus of about seven species, several of which are divided into subspecies. These snakes have never become popular with snake-keepers, which is unfortunate since they are easy to keep and feed, and breeding should not present difficulties. However, several of the species have the reputation of being aggressive and snappy, and it must be admitted that the adults of most species are rather dull in colour (although juveniles are often pretty).

Their care is almost identical to that of the garter snakes to which they are closely related, but they rarely if ever take earthworms and must be fed on fish or amphibians. They require a temperature of about 25°C (77°F) during the summer, lowered to 15–20°C (59–68°F) during the winter. All species are live-bearing, with litter sizes which may approach 100 (e.g. in *N. cyclopion*), but which are usually between 20 and 50.

Availability: Water snakes are readily available through importers, although they often arrive in poor condition. Captive-bred animals are rarely offered.

24. Mangrove Water Snake, *Nerodia fasciata compressicauda*, an example of a large group of North American semi-aquatic 'water' snakes.

Opheiodryas aestivus   Rough Green Snake

Size: to 75 cm (30 in)
Range: eastern North America

This pretty little snake is unmarked bright green above, paler green or white below. The head and body are slender and its movements are exceedingly graceful. Although it is not truly arboreal, it climbs well among low vegetation, etc., where it is well camouflaged.

In captivity it should be given a relatively large cage, and a group of four or more animals make an excellent display. This is one of the few species of snakes which appreciate a fairly natural set-up. The substrate may consist of dead leaves, bracken, pebbles, etc., which should be kept dry, and a lattice of dead branches will encourage the snakes to climb and bask under a light. Living plants, e.g. ivy, may be included, although these should be contained in small pots rather than planted directly into the substrate. A temperature of about 25°C (77°F) is required, and this may be provided by a light bulb or by bottom heat. The species is entirely insectivorous in diet, and takes crickets and locust hoppers, which it hunts with rapid darting movements, and waxworms, as well as insects that may be obtained by sweeping herbage with a butterfly net. Although I can find no records of captive breeding, this species would almost certainly require a cooling-off period of two to three months at 15°C (59°F) before this occurs. Clutches average about 5 eggs; it is important to isolate females before laying since any uneaten insects in the cage will attack the eggs.

Availability: Wild-caught specimens are frequently available at a reasonable price, but this species is not regularly bred in captivity.

Note: a similar species, *Opheodryas vernalis*, the smooth green snake, is smaller and much less adaptable to captive conditions than this one.

Rhinocheilus lecontei   Longnosed Snake (Colour Plate 28)

Size: to about 75 cm (30 in)
Range: South-western United States and adjacent parts of Mexico

This desert species is strikingly marked with broad black saddles on a cream background. Between each black saddle is a variable amount of red speckling, appearing as a solid secondary saddle on some specimens. Note that the black areas do not encircle the body as in the tri-coloured kingsnakes, and the saddles contain white flecks in the flank region. The head is narrow, and the snout pointed.

This snake requires a hot, dry cage, to 30°C (86°F), and a hide-box. Although it appears primarily to eat lizards in the wild, some specimens adapt to a diet of rodents, while in others it is necessary to disguise the smell by rubbing a dead lizard over the mouse. This species does not appear to have been bred in captivity, but it would almost certainly require a cooling-off period before doing so.

Genus *Tantilla*   Black-headed Snakes

North and Central America

The black-headed snakes, of which there are about 50 species in all, are superficially very similar. Growing to a maximum of about 40 cm (16 in), they are slender brown snakes with a black 'cap' on their heads. They are secretive in their habits, usually being found beneath rocks, logs or leaves, although they become active at night. Although not popular with keepers, their habits are poorly known and much information could be obtained from captives.

They are easily kept in small plastic boxes with 1 cm (in) or so of peat/sand mixture. A small flat stone should be placed at one end, and a water dish at the other. The substrate beneath this should be sprayed occasionally. Black-headed snakes appear to eat only invertebrates, consisting of small spiders, crickets, centipedes, etc. In captivity they will live indefinitely on a diet of cricket nymphs and waxworms.

There are no records of captive breeding, and it seems likely that this has not been achieved, through lack of interest. Data from wild specimens indicates that they lay a small number of elongated eggs.

Genus *Thamnophis*   Garter and Ribbon Snakes (Plate 25)

North and Central America

Garter snakes are probably among the most commonly kept species, especially by beginners, and very many experienced keepers and breeders will have gained their initiation on a garter snake, collected locally or purchased cheaply from a pet shop. Among the virtues which account for their popularity with beginners are their gentle nature (usually!), dietary preferences, and tolerance of a wide range of temperatures. However, despite the apparent ease of maintaining these snakes, problems do arise, and regular breeding is by no means a common event.

25.   Western Ribbon Snake, *Thamnophis proximus*, a close relative of the garter snakes, which does well in captivity provided that a plentiful supply of small fish can be obtained.

A range of the more commonly available species and subspecies is given below, but the general care is common to all. Garter and ribbon snakes are active, diurnal species which require relatively large cages. Temperatures should be in the region of 25°C (77°F) during the summer, but reduced to 15°C (59°F) or less during the winter, especially if breeding is to be attempted. A water container in which the snakes can soak should be included, but it is vitally important that this is kept only half-filled in order to avoid spillage, since all species are prone to blisters and scale-rot if kept on a damp substrate. A hide-box should be provided, although this is not always used, especially by long-term, tame individuals.

The greatest problem in keeping these species arises from their diet. A few of the larger species will eat rodents, which are ideal. However, the majority will only eat fish, amphibians and earthworms (ribbon snakes rarely, if ever, take earthworms). These items are not especially nutritious and, as a consequence, garter snakes should be fed more often than many colubrids, at least twice a week when active. Furthermore, there is a problem associated with the feeding of certain types of fish, for instance whitebait, other oily fish and possibly other types, which contain the enzyme thiaminase. This substance effectively destroys Vitamin B1, so rendering the snakes deficient, with consequent loss of balance, paralysis and eventual death. If fish are to be used as the staple diet, therefore, it is necessary to denature the thiaminase before feeding, and this is best achieved by heating small pieces to a temperature of 80°C (176°F) in water for about five minutes. Following this it is a good practice, though probably not essential, to fortify the fish with a vitamin and mineral supplement, such as Reptovit. In order to avoid calcium and phosphorus deficiencies, it is also important either to ensure that each piece of fish contains a section of bone, or to add further supplements in the form of powdered cuttlefish bone or a commercial calcium:phosphorus preparation. Snakes fed largely on live fish, e.g. goldfish or minnows, or amphibians do not require such treatment.

Breeding seems to be more likely to occur if the animals are kept in small groups rather than as single pairs. Such groups can contain one or two males and up to ten females, and these should be kept permanently together. If the animals are cooled down during the winter, mating takes place as soon as they become active again in the spring. The gestation period varies according to temperature, but is normally about four to five months. Pregnant females spend much of their time basking, and become noticeably swollen towards the end of gestation, and I have found it beneficial to include a small area of slightly moist sphagnum moss in the cage, where the female will usually give birth. The young are very small, and may easily escape from the cage unless all doors, etc. are a good fit;

failing this, the female should be moved to a plastic box before giving birth. The young shed their skins almost as soon as they are born and will begin to feed straight away. Earthworms are most readily accepted, but the young can usually be weaned onto small strips of fish without too much trouble. They grow rapidly and have been known to reproduce in the year following their birth.

The following list of species and subspecies represents those which are available with a reasonable degree of frequency. Several others will obviously be available to persons living in North America where one or more will almost certainly occur locally. Care of all garter and ribbon snakes, however, is basically similar. Unfortunately, there are no regular sources of captive-bred garter or ribbon snakes, although it may be possible to locate persons with young for sale through the various societies.

Thamnophis butleri   Butler's Garter Snake

A small species, rarely growing to more than 70 cm (28 in), Butler's garter snake is dark brown or black with three well-defined yellow or orange stripes. It apparently feeds almost entirely on earthworms.

Very little information is available on the care of this species in captivity: one record mentions a litter of 12 born to a female which was pregnant when captured.

Thamnophis elegans   Western Terrestrial Garter Snake

This is a highly variable garter snake, both in appearance and habits. As a rule, the dorsal stripe is cream or yellow and well defined, but the lateral stripes are vague. The area between the stripes is usually pale with darker blotches, but the colour may vary from brick-red (*T. e. terrestris*) to black (*T. e. elegans*). This is a large form which can grow to 100 cm (40 in) in length, and some subspecies, e.g. *T. e. terrestris*, will take small rodents readily, but others are not nearly so easy to feed.

Although this species has a potentially large litter size, the only records of captive breeding which have been found record litters of 6 and 7 young, which ate fish and earthworms.

KEY REFERENCE:
Butler, R. (1985). 'The captive care and breeding of *Thamnophis elegans terrestris*'. *Herptile* 10(2):34–38. (Comprising the proceedings of the 1985 IHS symposium.)

Thamnophis marcianus   Chequered Garter Snake (Colour Plate 29)

A very attractive species, being ochre or putty-coloured with a cream or yellow vertebral stripe and two rows of alternating black blotches on either side.

This species adapts very well to captivity, although its litter size is rather small,[14] and 9 having been recorded under these conditions.

Thamnophis radix   Plains Garter Snake

A small species, growing to about 70 cm (28 in), with a bright orange stripe down the centre of the back and a blue or greenish one on each flank. The area between may be matt black, or pale with black blotches; the subspecies *haydeni* differs from the nominate one in that these black blotches are smaller and more numerous.

This species generally does well in captivity and has been bred on several occasions. Litters range from 5–58 in number, born in July or August, and the neonates measure 15–18 cm (6–7 in) in length.

KEY REFERENCE:

Zwart, P. and van Ham, B. (1980). 'Keeping, breeding and raising garter snakes, *Thamnophis radix*'. In: Townson, S. et al (eds.). *The Care and Breeding of Captive Reptiles*, British Herpetological Society.

Thamnophis sauritus   Eastern Ribbon Snake

Ribbon snakes are more elongated than the closely related garter snakes, but are otherwise similar, being marked with the three longitudinal stripes which are characteristic of the genus. In this species, the stripes are yellow, orange or blue and well defined. The remainder of the snake is dark brown or black.

Care of ribbon snakes is similar to that of the garter snakes except that they will not take earthworms, and must therefore be fed on fish or amphibians. Litter sizes tend to be small, commonly 4 or 5, and the slender young measure 25–30 cm (10–12 in).

Thamnophis sirtalis   Common Garter Snake

This species is divided into a number of subspecies which between them range over almost the entire United States and into Canada. Despite its collective name, this genus contains some of the rarest North American reptiles as well as some of the commonest. The species is highly variable, but is basically dark brown, black or olive with three white, cream or yellow stripes. The areas between the stripes may be spotted with black.

26. Florida Garter Snake, *Thamnophis sirtalis similis*, an attractive form of
the Eastern Garter Snake in which the whole body is suffused with blue.

The most distinct subspecies are:

T. s. concinnus, red-spotted garter snake, which has distinctive bars of red
or pink between the stripes, which may be bluish. The top of the head
is often red.

T. s. tetrataenia, San Francisco garter snake, a spectacular species in
which the dorsal stripe is yellow, flanked by stripes of bright red. The top
of the head is also red. This subspecies is the rarest snake in North
America and is totally protected (Colour Plate 30).

T. s. parietalis, red-sided garter snake, in which the area between the
stripes has red bars, most of the colour being confined to the interstitial
skin between the scales. This subspecies is exceedingly common in some
areas and is the one most frequently met with in pet stores.

T. s. similis, Florida garter snake, which is a larger than average form,
with a bluish wash over the entire snake, but most noticeable on the
stripes (Plate 26).

T. s. sirtalis, eastern garter snake, a variable subspecies which is typically
black or dark brown with three yellow stripes, but which may also be
greenish, grey or even pinkish. In certain northern parts of its range this
subspecies is prone to melanism and all or most of some populations are
totally black (Colour Plate 31).

At least six other subspecies have been described, but are rarely seen in
captivity.

CHAPTER 12

Venomous Snakes

This chapter deals with the snakes of two families, all of which are venomous to some degree. These are the cobras (Elapidae) and the vipers (Viperidae), the latter being clearly separated into the 'true' vipers, subfamily Viperinae, and the pit vipers, subfamily Crotalinae (sometimes regarded as a separate family, the Crotalidae). The chapter is therefore divided into three sections.

Unfortunately, information on the care and breeding of these species is not as comprehensive as it might be. Recent restrictions on keeping them, for reasons of public safety, have resulted in far fewer specimens maintained, and for the same reason, the incentive to breed them has also disappeared since disposal of the young is often difficult. Therefore, although many species undoubtedly have been, and are being, bred in small numbers, data has not been easy to obtain.

The general care of venomous snakes does not vary in principle from that of other snakes, save that special precautions must be taken with respect to handling and housing. Suggested below are the basic precautions which should be observed.

PRECAUTIONS FOR KEEPING POISONOUS SNAKES

This chapter deals with poisonous snakes, the cobras and the vipers. Both these families contain species which may concern the snake-keeper and breeder, and several of them make highly interesting and rewarding subjects for captivity. However, there are obvious drawbacks and risks in keeping snakes of this kind, and the following remarks are intended to minimise these. It is essential, in the first instance, to ascertain whether there is existing legislation that restricts the keeping of such species and also stipulates the conditions under which permissible kinds are maintained. Notwithstanding the guidelines given here, it should go without saying that all legal obligations must be met.

The hazard of snakebite varies from species to species in both the severity of a potential bite, and in the likelihood of being bitten. However, all venomous species should be treated with respect, and situations which involve risk of snakebite should always be avoided; the bite of many 'relatively harmless' species can cause permanent damage to muscle or nervous tissue, and may prove fatal to the very young, very old, or persons suffering from otherwise non-fatal diseases. It is also worth noting that the majority of bites from captive snakes can be put down to a casual attitude towards handling and/or insufficient planning in respect of cage design, etc.

A complication in the treatment of snakebite is that few medical staff will have had experience in the treatment of non-local species, and since the literature regarding snakebite often gives conflicting advice, treatment is not always as straightforward as may be hoped.

Precautions fall into two categories, those to be taken in order to avoid a bite, and those which should be taken in the event of a bite.

Bites are most easily avoided by minimising handling and by careful design and management of the cages and the room in which they are kept:

Most importantly, the room should be as large as possible, with the minimum of clutter. This means that the floor should be kept clear of cages, buckets and other paraphernalia, which are best housed on shelves, in wall-mounted cupboards, or clipped to the wall. If the building is old, ensure that all gaps between floorboards, around pipework, etc. are blocked up.

The cage should be strongly built and placed on a firm and solid base. There should be provision for a padlock on the door(s) of the cage and this should be kept fastened at all times except when the cage is being serviced.

If possible, a second person, who is familiar with emergency procedures, should be present in the room when cages are opened. For more intimate operations, such as force-feeding, drug administration, etc., this precaution is absolutely essential.

The nearest doctor and/or hospital should be notified that venomous snakes are kept, and appropriate arrangements concerning procedures should be made with them.

The appropriate anti-venene should be available in the same building as the snakes. It must be refrigerated, well-labelled (especially if more than one type is stocked), and renewed as soon as its shelf life has expired. It should not be administered by the herpetologist or other non-medical persons, except in cases of dire emergency, but should be taken to the hospital by, or with, the victim. For emergencies, a few syringes of appropriate capacity and needles should be kept with the anti-venene. A notice on each cage should give the name of the species, location of the anti-venene, and name, address and telephone number of the doctor or hospital where treatment can be carried out. This label should be detachable, and should accompany the patient in the event of a bite.

The following additional rules should be observed when working with venomous snakes:

If a snake escapes and cannot be easily and immediately recaptured, kill it.

Never open a cage containing venomous snakes if you are tired or have been drinking alcohol.

Never open a cage unless the animal(s) have been located, or at least until you are certain that they are not in the vicinity of the door.

Never reach over or past a snake into the cage with bare hands. Above all, do not lose sight of the snake while the cage is being serviced, unless you *know* that it is in its hide-box.

When the cage is to be completely cleaned, transfer the snake before starting work.

Never touch or handle venomous snakes with bare hands unless it is absolutely essential; most snakes can be moved with a snake-hook, or by being persuaded into a transfer cage.

If a bite does occur, *don't panic!* Sit or lie down – unnecessary movement will only cause the venom to work its way around the blood system more quickly. If there is a second person available, he or she should carry out all the following instructions. If not, they should be done quickly but not hurriedly by the patient:

Return the snake to its cage if it can be caught safely, otherwise kill it.

Notify the local doctor or hospital by telephone.

Remove label from cage and pin to patient's clothing.

Remove anti-venene from refrigerator.

Drive patient to hospital, or await ambulance.

IN EMERGENCIES ONLY, first aid measures may be taken. These consist of applying a tourniquet above the bite, remembering to loosen it every ten to fifteen minutes, and injecting one vial of anti-venene as follows:

Clean outside of vial with alcohol, if possible.

Fill syringe with anti-venene.

Hold syringe vertically and drive out all air.

Clean skin with alcohol, if possible.

Inject anti-venene into muscle near affected area. The syringe should be firmly inserted well into the muscle, and the plunger pushed in slowly and steadily. If resistance is felt, pause and resume injecting more slowly. When the syringe is empty, withdraw the needle, and apply light pressure over the site of the injection for a few seconds to prevent leakage of anti-venene.

HANDLING VENOMOUS SNAKES

As stated above, there should be little or no need ever to handle a venomous snake with bare hands. Snakes can be moved from cage to cage by using a hook or, if necessary, a grab-stick or noose. A transfer cage is of great value, and consists of a small box, similar to a hide-box, with an entrance which can be closed once the snake is inside. This operation should be carried out with a snake-hook or, preferably, from outside the cage by means of some remote-control arrangement.

There are occasions, however, when handling is unavoidable, for instance if a snake has to be force-fed, given drugs, or have pieces of unshed skin, such as the spectacles, removed. Several techniques have been described for the safe execution of these procedures, one of the best involving the use of a length of clear acrylic tubing (*see* Fig. 16). This must be of slightly larger diameter than the snake, which is forced to crawl into it. One or more apertures are cut in the tube for access to various parts of the snake, and when these are in the correct position in relation to the snake, its tale is grasped and manipulations, such as injections, etc. can be carried out through the apertures. This method requires two people, one to restrain the snake while the other performs the manipulations, and the operation of getting the snake into the tube must be carefully executed (a plastic funnel is often useful). Force-feeding can also be carried out safely with this apparatus, in which case there will be no need to cut apertures in the tube. The snake is allowed to crawl up the tube until its head is almost, but not quite, out of the other end.

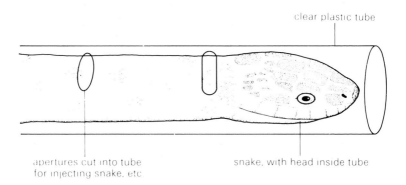

clear plastic tube

apertures cut into tube
for injecting snake, etc

snake, with head inside tube

Fig. 16. A safe way of restraining a venomous snake during probing, force-feeding or the administration of drugs. The snake is allowed to crawl into the tube but its tail is grasped before its head emerges from the other end. For giving injections, etc., apertures cut in the tube allow access to various parts of the snake's body.

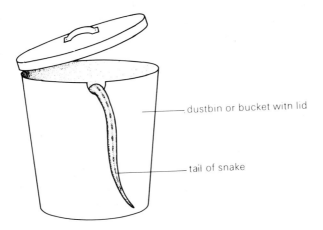

dustbin or bucket with lid

tail of snake

Fig. 17. A crude but effective method of restraining a venomous snake for probing. The snake is draped over the rim of the bucket so that its body rests in a suitable notch and its head is inside. The lid is then replaced and firmly held with a foot or by an assistant while the tail is grasped. Probing can then proceed quickly and without risk of being bitten.

Its tail is then held in the normal way and food pushed to the back of its throat. Swallowing will usually proceed voluntarily at this stage, the tube helping the process by keeping the snake's body straight.

If it is only necessary to gain access to the posterior half of the snake, when probing, for example, a simpler and safer method is to use a small plastic bucket with a notch of appropriate size cut into the rim (*see* Fig. 17). The snake is lifted by a hook into this notch, with the front half of its body inside the bucket and the tail outside. The lid of the bucket is now replaced, and light pressure applied, either with a foot or by a second person. The head is now safely confined to the bucket and a variety of operations can be carried out on the exposed portion. More detailed accounts of these methods are given in three papers listed in the bibliography (Gillingham et al. 1983, Murphy 1971, and Radcliffe 1975).

Family Elapidae – Cobras

Members of the cobra family are found throughout the tropical world, and contain many small and relatively harmless species as well as several of the more spectacularly dangerous ones. However, all those species commonly kept in captivity should be regarded as potentially lethal and the greatest care should be taken in their handling. Cobras, and their relatives the mambas, coral snakes, etc. are fast and unpredictable in their movements, whilst their venom is especially potent, often affecting the nervous system. They are difficult to handle with a snake-hook and, if handling is absolutely essential, this is best carried out with a clamp-stick or a noose-stick. Both these techniques, however, involve a certain degree of risk to the snake, and, where possible, catching boxes are to be preferred in every case.

Few species are kept, save as exhibits in zoos, where specimens are often maintained in solitary confinement.

Genus *Micrurus*   Coral Snakes

The coral snakes are confined to the New World. They are well known for their brilliant coloration, which consists typically of red, white and black rings, and which is usually regarded as a form of warning coloration, although its function is by no means certain. All are secretive burrowing species which feed largely on other snakes, lizards and amphisbaenids, and none of them are practical propositions for confinement.

A small amount of breeding data is available for the Texas coral snake, *M. fulvius tenere*. Matings are recorded for May, with clutches of 5–9 eggs being laid 37–50 days later. These hatched in 47–62 days, with the young measuring 18–24 cm (7–9 in). Their first food consisted of fence lizards

(*Sceloporus*). Further information can be obtained from the following paper:

Campbell, J. A. (1973). 'A captive hatching of *Micrurus fulvius tenere*.' *J. Herp.* 7(3):312–315.

Naja melanoleuca   Forest Cobra (Plate 27)

Size: to 250 cm (100 in)
Range: West and Central Africa

The forest cobra is a large dark species, usually brown on the head and front part of the body, becoming black towards the tail. The underside, displayed when the snake rears its body and spreads its hood, is cream, and the labial scales (lips) are also cream.

This species appears to be one of the more manageable species of cobras, most individuals adapting well to captivity and rarely showing the nervousness associated with several other members of the family. It requires a large cage, with a hide-box, preferably one which will double as a catching box. Temperatures of 25–30°C (77–86°F) are required, and mating appears to be more common if the snakes are given a slight cooling off period, to about 20°C (68°F) in the winter. The adults will eat mice, but feeding the young can be problematical.

Breeding data (from literature)

Time of mating:	April
Mating to egg-laying:	About 60 days
Number of eggs:	11–20 (average of 7 clutches, 14.9)
Incubation period:	80 days
Size of hatchlings:	34–44 cm (13–17 in)
First food:	Small snakes – also pink mice and small lizards occasionally

KEY REFERENCE:

Tryon, B. W. (1979). 'Reproduction in captive forest cobras, *Naja melanoleuca*.' *J. Herp.* 13(4):499–504.

Naja naja   Asiatic Cobra

Size: to about 180 cm (72 in)
Range   Asia

The Asiatic cobra, of which at least ten subspecies are recognised, is the one most frequently seen in zoos, etc. Its coloration varies from pale brown to black, usually without markings except for those on the hood,

27. Forest Cobra, *Naja melano-leuca*, one of the more easily managed cobras.

which may consist of a cream circle or of two such circles joined to form a 'spectacle'.

Care of this species is similar to that of *N. melanoleucus*. However, it is inclined to be somewhat more nervous than that species and plenty of security, in the form of a hide-box, must be provided. A fairly high humidity, at least 50%, should be maintained.

Breeding data (from literature)

Time of mating:	Various times throughout the year
Mating to egg-laying	Not known
Number of eggs:	17–21 (average of 4 clutches, 19.75)
Incubation period:	59–65 days
Size of young:	32–36 cm (12–14 in)
First food:	Pink mice, possibly rubbed with amphibians first

KEY REFERENCES:

Campbell, J. A. and Quinn, H. R. (1975). 'Reproduction in a pair of Asiatic cobras, *Naja naja*'. *J. Herp.* 9(2):229–233.

Hill, L. W. (1984). 'Captive reproduction of albino monocellate cobras, *naja naja kaouthia*'. *Proc. 8th Ann. Symp. on Captive Propagation and husbandry* 109–111.

Ophiophagus hannah   King Cobra

   Size: potentially to 500 cm (200 in), usually smaller
   Range: India and South-east Asia

This impressive cobra is uniformly coloured olive or yellowish-brown, except for juveniles, and adults from Burma and Thailand, which have lighter chevron markings. The hood of this species is noticeably narrower than that of the *Naja* species described and is unmarked.

In captivity, the king cobra has one serious drawback – it eats only other snakes. This obviously places a severe restriction on its use as a captive, although if this can be overcome it usually settles in well and is renowned for its 'intelligence' and placid disposition. It requires a constant temperature of 25–30°C (77–86°F) and a large cage with a hide-box. Some individuals have been persuaded to eat rodents which have been sewn into the sloughed skin of a snake, others will eat them if they are attached to the tail of a dead snake, so reducing the number of snakes which have to be used. If the food problem can be overcome, king cobras may breed.

Breeding data (from literature)

Time of mating:	December–May
Mating to egg-laying:	Not known
Number of eggs:	28–56 (average of 7 clutches, 38.1)
Incubation period:	63–76 days
Hatch-rate:	Not good, less than 50% overall
Size of hatchlings:	46–55 cm (18–22 in)
First food:	Small snakes

KEY REFERENCE:
   Burchfield, P. M. (1977). 'Breeding the king cobra, *Ophiophagus hannah*, at Brownsville Zoo'. *Int. Zoo Yb.*, 17:136–140.

Family Viperidae – Vipers

The vipers are a group of species comprising the subfamily Viperinae and are restricted to the Old World. They are replaced in the New World by the pit vipers, subfamily Crotalinae, which are dealt with later. All vipers differ from members of the cobra family in having fangs which are hinged and which can be folded back along the roof of the mouth. This enables the fangs to be longer than those of the cobras, and vipers typically stab with their fangs and then release their prey, tracking it down later by means of the tongue. All are heavy-bodied snakes with somewhat sluggish movements, although all can strike quickly. A relatively small number are kept in captivity.

Atheris chloroechis   African Bush Viper

   Size: to about 70 cm (28 in)
   Range: West Africa

Very little is known of the bush vipers, either in captivity or in the wild. These rare snakes are arboreal and inhabit remote areas of rain-forest in Central and West Africa.

A single report of reproduction in *A. chloroechis* is of interest since it is probably the only record of reproduction in the genus. Two females gave birth to 6 and 9 living young in March and April respectively, both litters resulting from wild matings, and both consisting entirely of females. The young were 16–19 cm (6–7 in) in length, and fed on small frogs, *Acris*, before graduating to pink mice.

KEY REFERENCE:
   Freed, P. (1986). '*Atheris chloroechis* (West African Bush Viper) Reproduction'. *Herp. Review* 17(2):47–48.

Bitis arietans   Puff Adder

   Size: to 100 cm (40 in)
   Range: Africa south of the Sahara

The broad spade-shaped head, typical of all snakes in the genus *Bitis*, is well demonstrated in this species. The overall colour is variable, most specimens being dark brown or dark grey with lighter, backward-pointing chevrons down the back.

In captivity this species requires a medium-sized cage with a hide-box and water bowl. It rarely climbs and height is not important. A temperature of 25–30°C (77–86°F) is required, although specimens from some parts of the range are very cold-tolerant. It eats mice readily and rarely presents problems to the keeper. Despite its normal lethargic disposition, this species strikes rapidly, and its bite may prove fatal.

Breeding is probably stimulated by a short period of cooler conditions in the winter. Adults of three years or more are sexually mature, and litters ranging from 1–58 (average of 9 litters, 23.8) are born during the summer. The newborn young eat pink mice, usually voluntarily.

Bitis gabonica   Gaboon Viper (Colour Plate 32)

   Size: potentially to 200 cm (80 in), usually smaller
   Range: forested regions of Africa

The Gaboon viper is arguably the world's most impressive venomous snake. Its immense size, particularly the broad head, and bizarre markings, immediately separate it from all other species. The colour and pattern are almost impossible to describe. Geometrical shapes of cream, brown, purple and pinkish-buff interlock on the flanks, a series of cream or buff rectangles is arranged along the dorsal midline, and the top of the head is of the same shade. A broad-based triangle of rich brown has its apex at the eye and its base along the upper jaw. The snout is adorned with a pair of small upturned 'horns', which are more prominent in the West African subspecies *B. g. rhinoceros*.

It seems that Gaboon vipers require a high humidity, but are often heavily infested with parasites. Until these are removed from the system the animals fail to put on weight, even though they may feed well at first, and eventually become emaciated and die. Therefore, prophylactic treatment with anti-helminthic drugs is indicated, unless the animals are captive-bred, which is unlikely. Other than this, their care is as described for the puff adder. This species delivers a huge amount of venom – victims of a serious bite rarely survive unless immediate medical aid is given. Therefore, despite its tractable nature, risks should never be taken.

Breeding has only been achieved on a few occasions, mostly within the natural range of the species. Litters are large, 43–53 having been recorded, with an estimated gestation period of about 171 days. Adult males of 130 cm (52 in) and females of 180 cm (72 in) are sexually mature.

KEY REFERENCE:

Akester, J. (1980). 'Breeding gaboon vipers, *Bitis gabonica gabonica*, in captivity.' In: Townson, S. et al, *The Care and Breeding of Captive Reptiles*, 63–68. British Herpetological Society, London.

Cerastes cerastes Desert Horned Viper (Colour Plate 33)

Size: to 60 cm (24 in)
Range: North Africa

This species of viper is a confirmed desert species, often living on loose, wind-blown sand, where it moves by sidewinding. Individuals are coloured to match the substrate on which they are living and therefore vary from pale yellow to brown or grey. A series of darker blotches, which may be in the form of crossbars, runs down the back. The most distinctive feature of this species is the presence of a horn over each eye.

Horned vipers usually thrive in captivity, requiring a temperature of 25–30°C (77–86°F) and a dry substrate, which may be of silver sand if the animals are on display. They eat rodents readily. Although their venom is not especially potent, they can be irascible and should be treated with respect.

Breeding appears to have been achieved only rarely. This species is unusual among vipers in that eggs are laid, clutches of 15–18 having been recorded. For some unknown reason, these usually spoil before they hatch. No further information is available.

Echis coloratus   Carpet Viper

Size: to 80 cm (3 in)
Range: Middle East

A highly variable species, which ranges from dark brown to buff, and may be reddish or greenish according to the geology of its habitat. A series of alternate dark and light blotches runs along the back, although again there is variation. The scales of this species are heavily keeled, and the snake rubs these together in order to produce a rasping sound.

Care of this species in captivity is similar to that of the desert horned viper (above), but it is far more dangerous. It also lays eggs, although breeding is rarely attempted.

Breeding data (from literature)

Time of mating:	Not known
Mating to egg-laying:	Not known
Number of eggs:	1–12 (average of 10 clutches, 6.7)
Incubation period:	40–52 days, typically 47 days at 28°C (82°F)
Hatch-rate:	About 75% overall; a case of 2 young in 1 egg has been reported
Size of hatchlings:	29–42 cm (11–16 in)
First food:	Pink mice

KEY REFERENCE:

Goode, M. (1979). 'Notes on captive reproduction in *Echis colorata*'. *Herp. Review* 10(3):94.

The species *Echis carinatus*, also known as the carpet viper, is very similar in appearance and habits. There is no information on the care or breeding of this snake in captivity, but it can safely be assumed that it is similar to that of the present species.

Vipera ammodytes   Sand Viper, Nose-horned Viper (Colour Plate 34)

Size: to 90 cm (36 in)
Range: South-east Europe and South-west Asia

The nose-horned viper is the largest and most imposing of the European *Vipera* species. In common with most other Europoean vipers, its markings consist of a vertebral zigzag, which is usually black but may be dark brown or grey. Occasionally, the line is not continuous but consists of a series of ovals. The ground colour varies, and may be light brown, grey or reddish; there is greater contrast between the markings in males than in females. The most obvious distinguishing feature is the prominent nose-horn, consisting of a number of scales, which protrudes from the snout.

This species is not difficult to care for. It requires warm, dry accommodation at about 25°C (77°F), and a hide-box. It eats mice readily. Its venom is more potent than that of any other European vipers but is not often fatal. Breeding has been achieved, but records are scant. Mating occurs in the spring, and the live young, numbering from 2–9 (average of 5 litters, 6.4) are born from July to September. They will take pink mice straight away.

Vipera aspis   Asp

> Size: to about 60 cm (24 in)
> Range: Western and Central Europe

A variable species, but identifiable by its snout, which is distinctly upturned, though lacking a horn. The markings on the body consist of a vertebral line which may be in a zigzag arrangement, but may also consist of separate crossbars or of a straight or slightly wavy dark line. The ground colour also varies, from cream to brown or grey. Totally black individuals occur, especially in mountainous regions.

The asp requires a medium-sized cage with a hide-box. It feeds readily on small mice. A temperature of around 25°C (77°F) suits it, although it is tolerant of much lower temperatures (especially individuals from mountain ranges). However, it is not essential to cool it down in order to induce breeding. Specimens which are kept permanently warm will breed every 8–10 months. Normally, breeding takes place in the spring.

Breeding data (from literature)

> Time of mating: March–May
> Gestation period: 88–90 days
> Number of young: 5–9 (average of 12 litters, 7.2)
> Size of neonates: 20–22 cm (8–8 in)
> First food: Pink mice, small lizards

KEY REFERENCES:

Naulleau, G. (1973a). 'Reproduction twice in one year in a captive viper (*Vipera aspis*)'. *Brit. J. Herpetol.* 5(1):353–357.

Naulleau, G. (1973b). 'Rearing the asp viper, *Vipera aspis*, in captivity'. *Int. Zoo Yb.* 13:108–111.

Vipera lebetina   Blunt-nosed Viper

Size: to 100 cm (40 in), occasionally larger
Range: South-west Asia, North-West Africa and Europe (Cyclades Islands)

The markings of this species consist of a row of brown blotches on each flank and two rows, often joined, along the dorsal mid-line. These blotches are not very distinct from the ground colour of pale brown or greyish-brown, and some individuals are more or less uniform in coloration.

Care of this species is as for *V. ammodytes*. However, it is unusual in being an egg-layer. Breeding is induced by cooling the snakes to about 15°C (59°F) during the winter.

Breeding data (from literature)

Time of mating:	March–April
Mating–egg-laying:	51–77 days
Number of eggs:	5–8 (average of 3 clutches, 6.7)
Incubation period:	37–48 days
Hatch-rate:	Infertile eggs are recorded for each of the above clutches
Size of hatchlings:	19 cm (7 in)
First food:	Not known, possibly lizards

Vipera russelli   Russell's Viper

Size: to 150 cm (60 in)
Range: India, South-east Asia

This dangerous species shows little resemblance to the European vipers. Its markings consist of a series of dark brown oval markings on each flank and along the dorsal mid-line. Each is edged with white, and the ground colour is usually brown but may be olive or yellowish.

The species requires a large cage and a temperature of 25–30°C (77–86°F). It feeds on rodents and rarely presents difficulties. It has been bred only occasionally; 2 clutches, of 12 and 26 eggs, are recorded, but there is no further information.

Other *Vipera* species

There are several other species of *Vipera* in Europe and the Middle East which make good captives, but which are, on the whole, a neglected group of snakes. Species such as *V. xanthina*, the Ottoman viper, and *V. palaestinae*, the Palestine viper, tend to be large, heavy-bodied species and fairly dangerous, whereas *V. berus*, the adder, *V. latastei*, Lataste's viper, and *V. kasnakovi*, the Caucausus viper (Colour Plate 35), are smaller and relatively innocuous. All these species require similar care to that given for the nose-horned viper, although *V. berus* is far more cold-tolerant and requires a period of complete hibernation during the winter. All have been kept successfully by small numbers of specialist collectors, and several have bred in captivity, although details are lacking. A further species, *V. ursinii*, the meadow viper, has a restricted range in various European mountain ranges and is totally protected.

Family Crotalidae – Pit Vipers

The pit vipers are contained in the subfamily Crotalinae, a branch of the viper family, Viperidae. They are distinct from the other branch of the family (Viperinae) by virtue of the heat-sensitive pits which are situated between the eye and the nostril. These unique organs enable them to detect and strike accurately at warm-blooded prey, even in total darkness, an ability which it is well to remember when carrying them in snake-bags! Their distribution is divided between the Americas and Asia, with relatively few genera but many species. In addition to the well-known rattlesnakes, the subfamily contains a number of attractive and interesting species which are worthy of a place in the specialist collection. Obviously, all these species are venomous, many of them dangerously so, and the precautions given at the beginning of this chapter apply.

Basic care and breeding vary from species to species but, in general, these snakes adapt well to captivity and have fairly placid dispositions. However, their rather ponderous locomotion should not be regarded as typical of all their movements as these snakes strike incredibly fast, often to the side. Like other vipers, their venom is not so potent, drop for drop, as that of the cobras, but they deliver a much larger dose, and their fangs are long.

Agkistrodon contortrix Copperhead (Plate 28)

Size: to about 100 cm (40 in)
Range: Eastern North America

28. Copperhead, *Agkistrodon contortrix*, an attractive and tractable pit viper, which adapts well to captive conditions.

The copperhead, of which three subspecies are recognised, is, in the opinion of many people, one of the most beautifully marked snakes in the world. Eleven to twenty wide bands of rich orange-brown cross a ground colour of pale tan or pinkish-cream. These bands expand slightly on the flanks and the exact number varies somewhat from one subspecies to another, as does the shade of colour. *A. c. pictigaster*, the Trans-Pecos copperhead, is usually regarded as the most handsome.

Copperheads are not difficult to care for, and are usually docile snakes. Furthermore, their bite is not especially dangerous, few fatalities ever having been recorded. They require a medium-sized cage with a hide-box, a temperature of 25°C (77°F) and a diet of rodents. For display purposes, a scattering of dead leaves over the floor of the cage shows off their disruptively camouflaged markings to perfection. Breeding is induced by lowering the temperature to about 15°C (59°F) for three months in the winter. Although mating can occur at almost any time of the year, fertilisation apparently takes place only during the spring, sometimes by sperm stored from the previous autumn.

Breeding data (from literature and John Muir)

Time of mating: March–October (see above)
Gestation period: 150–200 days
Number of young: 4–11 (average of 9 litters, 6.2)

161

Size of neonates: 24–26 cm (9–10 in)
    First food: Pink mice. Also insects, small lizards, etc.

Agkistrodon piscivorus Water Mocassin or Cottonmouth

    Size: to 120 cm (48 in)
  Range: South-eastern United States

A black or dark brown snake with several wide bands of lighter colour, which are fairly distinct in young specimens but often completely obscured in adults. A pale line passes through the eye in some specimens, notably those from Florida (subspecies *conanti*), but is an unreliable characteristic. The common name of 'cottonmouth' stems from their habit of gaping widely if approached, and displaying the white lining to their mouth. They are almost always aggressive.

Because of their dull appearance and aggressive disposition, mocassins are rarely kept in captivity. They require similar treatment to the previous species, but will eat fish and amphibians in addition to rodents. There is little information on breeding, save that 7–10 young are born in summer.

Bothrops schlegeli Eyelash Viper (Plate 29)

    Size: to about 75 cm (30 in)
  Range: Central America and extreme northern South America

This species is an arboreal pit viper with a prehensile tail. It is highly variable in coloration and may be olive-green, bright green, yellow or orange. Its most distinctive feature, from which its name derives, is the arrangement of pointed scales protruding from above the eyes.

Care of these rain-forest snakes calls for special arrangements. They should be given a tall cage with branches on which to rest, and regular, if possible daily, light spraying of the animals is essential, as they probably drink mainly from drops of water which collect in their coils. The use of natural spectrum fluorescent lights, e.g. True-light or Vita-lite appears to be beneficial. A temperature of 25–30°C (77–86°F) should be provided throughout the year, and their diet consists of mice, lizards and frogs.

No special stimuli appear to be necessary to induce mating. Females will breed more than once each year, the shortest recorded interval between litters being seven months and ten days (Blody, 1983). Under captive conditions this species becomes sexually mature in three to four years.

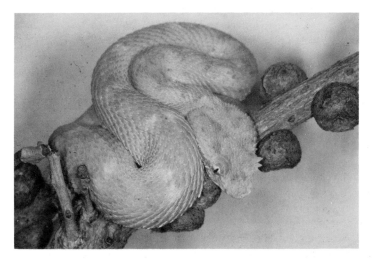

29. Eyelash Viper, *Bothrops schlegeli*, an arboreal pit viper from South America which needs special treatment if it is to thrive in captivity. This species is highly variable, the yellow form being one of several.

Availability: One of the most desirable of the pit vipers, this species is listed from time to time but prices are high. Captive-breeding does not yet occur regularly enough to meet the demand.

Breeding data (from literature)

Time of mating:	Any time of the year
Gestation period:	120–150 days, but often appears longer due to sperm retention
Number of young:	6–22 (average of 15 litters, 11.5)
Mortality rate:	Stillbirths frequent
Size of young:	Highly variable, ranging from 10 cm (4 in) in large litters to 21 cm (8 in). Typically about 18 cm (7 in)
First food:	Small frogs, pink mice later

KEY REFERENCES:

Blody, D. A. (1983). 'Notes on the reproductive biology of the eyelash viper, *Bothrops schlegeli*, in captivity'. *Herp. Review* 14(2):45–46.

Love, W. B. and Love, K. V. (1979). 'Notes on an unsuccessful eyelash viper breeding project'. *Proc. 3rd Ann. Symp. on Captive Propagation and Husbandry*, 69–72.

Other species of *Bothrops*, all of which have been bred at least once in captivity, are *B. alternatus, asper, moojeni, nasutus, nigroviridis, nummifer,* and *undulatus*. Recorded litters, which are few in number, ranged from 6–12, but additional data is lacking. All these species are Central or South American rain-forest snakes and their maintenance can be expected to be similar to that of *B. schlegeli*, but note that not all are arboreal.

Crotalus atrox   Western Diamondback Rattlesnake (Colour Plate 36)

Size: to 200 cm (80 in)
Range: South-western North America

An impressive rattlesnake, whose overall colour varies according to local conditions: commonly grey or brown, but sometimes reddish, buff or bluish-grey. The markings consist of darker, light-edged diamonds, touching one another and running down the back. The tail is always banded in black and white.

This rattlesnake is common, both in the wild and in snake collections. It thrives in captivity and is almost ridiculously easy to breed. It requires a large cage, a warm temperature of 25–30°C (77–86°F), and a diet of mice or rats. In order to induce breeding it should be cooled to 15–20°C (59–68°F) during the winter.

Availability: Although a popular exhibit in zoos, this species is not often kept by private snake-keepers, being too common and rather unattractive in appearance compared with several of the other, smaller species of rattlesnake. Obtaining specimens, either captive-bred or wild, should not present any great difficulty. An albino strain is also available.

Breeding data (from literature)

Time of mating:	March–May
Gestation period:	100–150 days
Number of young:	2–37 (average of 11 litters, 13.7)
Size of neonates:	24–33 cm (9–13 in)
First food:	Pink mice

Crotalus cerastes   Sidewinder (Colour Plate 37)

Size: to about 60 cm (24 in), occasionally larger
Range: South-western United States and adjacent parts of Mexico

The most distinctive characteristic of this species is the pair of 'horns' above the eyes, making it superficially similar to its African namesake,

Cerastes cerastes, which lives in a comparable environment. The side-winding locomotion is also common to both species. In other respects, the sidewinder is highly variable; the ground colour usually matches exactly the substrate on which it is living, and the spots and blotches on the back enhance this camouflage.

In captivity the sidewinder may be kept on an artificial substrate such as newspaper, but is seen to better advantage on sand or stones. It requires a daytime temperature of 25–30°C (77–86°F) but this may be reduced during the night. It feeds on small rodents and lizards, and captives appear to prefer the latter. It can be snappy, but its venom is not particularly potent. Although this species has undoubtedly been bred, there are no data available.

Crotalus durissus   Cascabel

    Size: to 150 cm (60 in)
    Range: most of Central and South America

A variable species of which several subspecies are recognised. The pattern consists of a series of linked diamonds, edged in white and with pale centres.

This species is rarely kept in captivity, although there do not appear to be any serious problems in its maintenance. The small amount of data available suggests that 1–29 young (average 13.4) are born in May or June.

Crotalus vegrandis   Uracoan Rattlesnake

    Size: to 60 cm (24 in)
    Range: Venezuela

A speckled rattlesnake, being overall olive-brown or grey with a peppering of white or cream flecks on practically every scale.

Care of this species is straightforward. It requires a medium-sized cage, a temperature of 25–30°C (77–86°F) and a diet of mice. The species will begin to breed at less than two years of age, and females will produce litters at almost any time of the year, with an interval between litters of about nine months. John Muir of South Pittsburg, Tennessee, sums up the breeding of this species thus: 'It appears that the only prerequisite to successfully breeding *Crotalus vegrandis* is to have a pair and place them together.'

Availability: Captive-bred young of this species are frequently available.

Breeding data (from literature and J. Muir)

Time of mating: Throughout the year
Gestation period: 200–270 days
Number of young: 2–14 (average of 10 litters, 8.3)
Size of young: 22–28 cm (8–11 in)
First food: Pink mice

KEY REFERENCE:

Murphy, J. B., Mitchell, L. A. and Cooper, J. A. (1979). 'Miscellaneous notes on the reproductive biology of reptiles. III. The Uracoan rattlesnake, *Crotalus vegrandis*.' *J. Herp.* 13(3):373–374.

Several other species of rattlesnake are kept and occasionally bred in captivity. Although many details are lacking, the few breeding data which are available are given in abbreviated form (Plate 30):

Crotalus catalinensis – two litters, of 4 and 7, born in July and September, one after a gestation period of 147 days.

Crotalus enyo – two clutches, of 1 and 8, recorded, both born in September.

30. Mojave Rattlesnake, *Crotalus scutellatus*, a medium-sized desert rattler which can be maintained quite easily in captivity but which carries a dangerous and rapid-acting venom.

Crotalus horridus, Timber Rattlesnake – four clutches ranging from 4–14 are recorded, three of which were born in August.

Crotalus lepidus, Rock Rattlesnake – a single clutch of 6 is recorded.

Crotalus mitchelli, Speckled Rattlesnake – three clutches of 1, 6 and 7 recorded.

Crotalus unicolor, Arruba Island Rattlesnake – several litters of this endangered rattlesnake have been produced, ranging in size from 2–9 (average 3.9). A gestation period of about 240 days is indicated, and the young measure 23–29 cm (9–11 in).

Crotalus viridis, Western Rattlesnake – three clutches, of 5, 5 and 8 recorded, with a gestation period of about 240 days (subspecies *oreganus*).

These, and several other species of rattlers are kept in small numbers by specialist snake-keepers and breeders, as well as by zoos. Restrictions on the keeping of venomous snakes have undoubtedly stifled a great deal of enthusiasm for these species, which is regrettable since they are interesting and most adapt very well to captivity.

Genus *Trimeresurus*   Asian Pit Vipers

The Asian pit vipers include arboreal and terrestrial species, and in many ways their evolution has paralleled that of the South American *Bothrops* species. Most of the arboreal species, which are the most frequently encountered, are green in coloration although Wagler's, *T. wagleri*, is purplish-brown with an intricate pattern which may include yellow, white and red speckles. Their care in captivity, at least of those species most often kept, is usually quite straightforward. They require medium-sized cages which should be tall in the case of arboreal species, and fitted with branches. Humidity does not seem as critical as with the *Bothrops* species, but a temperature of 25–30°C (77–86°F) should be maintained throughout the year. Adults will normally eat small mice, but the young usually require frogs or fish to get them started. Bites from these species are rarely lethal, but are to be avoided since permanent damage to tissue can result.

The small amount of breeding data which is available is listed below. Note that sperm retention is well developed in this genus, making any attempt at recording gestation periods meaningless.

T. albolabris, White-lipped Pit Viper – litters of 1–18 (average of 5 litters, 6.5) are recorded born June–August. The young measure about 20 cm (8 in) in length and eat small frogs.

T. gramineus – litters of 3–37 (average of 6 litters, 14.7) recorded, born at various times of the year. Young measure 15–17 cm (6–6 in) in total length.

T. okinavensis – a single litter of 7 recorded.

T. popeorum, Pope's Pit Viper – a single litter of 7 recorded (Colour Plate 39).

T. purpuromaculata – a single litter of 7 recorded.

T. steineri – a single litter of 12 recorded.

Sources of Captive-Bred Snakes

In order to assist readers to locate captive animals of the species in which they are interested, listed below are a number of commercial and semi-commercial snake-breeding operations.

The list is by no means complete, and many other reliable breeders no doubt exist. Neither does inclusion on the list indicate unreserved recommendation.

Prospective buyers are strongly advised to visit breeders if at all possible before making purchases, since animals vary greatly in quality and coloration, etc. However, it must be said that those addresses which I have personally visited have left me most impressed with the standard of husbandry, and the fair way in which business has been conducted.

United States

ROBERT APPLEGATE, 1762 Peppervilla Drive, El Cajon, California 92021.

HENRY J. COHEN, 562 Hall Road, Elma, New York 14059.

BILL CORWIN, 2514 Alco, Dallas, Texas 75211.

WILLIAM B. GILLINGHAM, 1035 Middlefield Ave., Stockton, California 95 204.

STEPHEN HAMMACK, 3114 Westcliff Road, Forth Worth, Texas 76109.

MICHAEL W. HAMMOCK (Hammock Herpetological), Route #1, Wallace Road, Luttrell, Tennessee 37779.

TERRY HOWE, 656 Santa Coleta Court, Sunnyvale, California 94086.

BILL AND KATHY LOVE (GLADES HERPETOCULTURE), P.O. Box 643, Alva, Florida 33920.

JOHN H. MUIR, P.O. Box 723, South Pittsburg, Tennessee 37380.

STEVEN T. OSBORNE, 36009 96th Street East, Littlerock, California 93543.

LARRY ROUCH, P.O. Box 534, Stafford, Virginia 22554.

GARY SIPPERLEY (San Diego Reptile Breeders), 6747 Renkrib Avenue, San Diego, California 92119.

VINCE SCHEIDT, 6812 Syracuse Lane, San Diego, California 92122.

DAVID SORENSON, 6901 West Sheridan Avenue, Milwaukee, Wisconsin 53218.

TOM TAYLOR, 1433 W. Huntington Drive, Tempe, Arizona 85282.
ERNIE WAGNER, 354 North 76th, Seattle, Washington 98103.

Britain

RICHARD ALLEN, 8 The Broadway, Lambourn, Berkshire RG16 7XY, England.

DAVID BLATCHFORD, Bungalow No. 2, Kirkhill Cottages, St Quivox, Ayr, Ayrshire KA6 5HJ, Scotland.

RAYMOND A. HINE, P.O. Box 992, Wickford, Essex SS12 9EW, England.

MIKE NOLAN, 29 Rodney Close, New Malden, Surrey KT3 5AA, England.

APPENDIX II

Herpetological Societies

There are an increasing number of societies catering for the amateur and professional herpetologist. Not all of these encourage snake-keeping, but most publish journals and newsletters which contain information of interest to the snake-keeper. More importantly, they provide contact with other enthusiasts who will be willing to exchange information and buy or sell surplus captive-bred snakes.

Regrettably, names and addresses of secretaries have a habit of changing, making an accurate listing difficult and short-lived. However, the major societies, listed below, should all be able to provide up-to-date information regarding smaller, localised societies in the areas which their membership covers. Failing this, society details should be available from dealers, museums, libraries, etc.

Australasia

AUSTRALASIAN AFFILIATION OF HERPETOLOGICAL SOCIETIES, P.O. Box R307, Royal Exchange, Sydney, NSW, 2000, Australia. (Publication: *Herpetofauna*).

Europe

ASSOCIATION FOR THE STUDY OF REPTILES AND AMPHIBIANS, c/o Cotswold Wildlife Park, Burford, Oxon, England. (Publication: *Journal of the Association for the Study of Reptiles and Amphibians.*)

BRITISH HERPETOLOGICAL SOCIETY, c/o Zoological Society of London, Regent's Park, London NW1 4RY, England. (Publications: *British Journal of Herpetology; Bulletin of the British Herpetological Society.*)

DUTCH SNAKE SOCIETY, Secretary: Jaap Kooij, Langerveldweg 137, 2211 AG Noordwilkerhout, The Netherlands. (Publication: *Litteratura Serpentium.*)

INTERNATIONAL HERPETOLOGICAL SOCIETY, Secretary: Mr A. J. Mobbs, 65 Broadstone Avenue, Walsall, West Midlands, England. (Publication: *The Herptile.*)

United States

Note: Most states have at least one regional society for herpetologists, some have several. Although it is not possible to list these here, it will be relatively easy for enthusiasts to obtain the relevant addresses from dealers in reptiles, from a local zoological gardens or from public museums.

AMERICAN FEDERATION OF HERPETOCULTURISTS, P.O. Box 1131, Lakeside, California 92040. (Publication: *The Vivarium.*)

SOCIETY FOR THE STUDY OF REPTILES AND AMPHIBIANS. Treasurer and membership information: Henry C. Seibert, Department of Zoological and Biomedical Sciences, Ohio University, Ohio 45701. (Publications: *Journal of Herpetology; Herpetological Review.*)

Laws Pertaining to the Keeping of Snakes

Several laws have a bearing on the keeping of snakes, the most important of which are summarised below. Note, however, that the following information is intended for guidance only and the possession of current information, obtained by reference to the relevant authorities, is always desirable.

International Treaties

In recent years, two important conventions dealing with the protection of wildlife have been drawn up. Both have a direct bearing on the keeping of reptiles.

1) *Convention on International Trade in Endangered Species of Flora and Fauna* (CITES) 1973 – sometimes known as the 'Washington Convention'.

This convention (not ratified by the United Kingdom, but incorporated with modifications into the Endangered Species (Import and Export) Act 1976) sets out regulations whereby certain species which are considered to be endangered or threatened are protected through the co-operation of the party states by restricting their import and export.

The animals concerned are classed as 'threatened' (Appendix I), likely to become threatened (Appendix II), or subject to internal regulations in one or more of the party states. Import, export or re-export of the animals on these lists is possible only if import and export licences or permits are first obtained. These licences, where granted, are valid for one consignment within six months of issue and are applicable only provided that the animals are not obtained illegally, and that they are shipped in such a way as to minimise the risk of injury, damage to health, and cruelty.

Exceptions are made for animals bred in captivity (but if these are species normally listed in Appendix I, they are treated as though they were in Appendix II), animals loaned or donated between scientists or scientific institutions, and travelling zoos, circuses, etc.

Where trade with non-party states is involved, comparable documentation will be accepted in lieu of the usual import of export licences or permits.

The animals listed in the Appendices include several snakes, for example, all *Python* species.

2) *Convention on the Conservation of European Wildlife and Natural Habitats* 1979 – sometimes known as the 'Berne Convention'

Under this convention (not ratified by the United Kingdom, but incorporated with modifications into the Wildlife and Countryside Act 1981) the contracting parties (most of Europe) agree to co-operate in protecting important natural habitats and listed plants and animals. Exceptions may be made for various reasons including: education; re-population; and the keeping, on a small scale, of certain species under supervised conditions. In addition, the parties agree to control the introduction of non-native species.

Appendix I lists 'strictly protected' plants; Appendix II lists 'strictly protected' animals (including 11 snakes of which 6 are vipers); Appendix III lists 'protected' animals, and all snakes not listed in Appendix II are automatically included here.

British Laws

PET ANIMALS ACT 1951

Under this Act it is illegal to sell animals except from premises which are registered for that purpose by the local authority who will first appoint a vet to inspect them in order to ensure that they are suitable for accommodating animals in a humane manner, and that they meet certain other requirements. An exception may be made where the animals have been bred by the vendor.

DANGEROUS WILD ANIMALS ACT 1976

Under this Act nobody may keep a dangerous wild animal unless they have obtained a licence from the local authority. The licence application must specify the species and number of animals to be kept, and must be accompanied by a fee set by the local authority. The licence will only be granted provided that the applicant is aged 18 years or over, and is considered 'suitable'; that the authority is satisfied that the animal(s) will be placed in suitable accommodation and provided with adequate food, drink, bedding etc. Before a licence is issued, the premises will be inspected by a vet to ensure that the above conditions are met satisfactorily, and the applicant must also pay the fee for this inspection. In addition, the animals must remain at the specified premises and be kept only by the specified licence-holder and he must take out insurance against damage caused by the animal(s). Licences run for one year, and the premises may be inspected again at any time throughout the year.

Exceptions to the law are zoos, circuses, pet shops and premises registered for performing experiments on animals.

The snakes figuring on the list are: all Elapidae (Cobras, Kraits, Mambas, Coral Snakes, etc.) and Viperidae (Vipers and Rattlesnakes). In addition, a number of back-fanged colubrid snakes have been placed on the list. These include the following three species which have commonly been available through the pet trade: Mangrove Snake, *Boiga dendrophila*; Montpellier Snake, *Malpolon monspessulanus*; Long-nosed Tree Snake, *Dryophis nasuta*.

ENDANGERED SPECIES (IMPORT AND EXPORT) ACT 1976

This Act incorporates the Washington Convention into British law (*see* above), and regulates the import and export of certain endangered and vulnerable species. It is re-enacted, with amendments, by the Wildlife and Countryside Act 1981 (*see* below). It states that the importation of listed species may only be carried out if an import licence is first obtained, and it may be necessary to have additional documentation from the exporting country. For animals imported without licences, i.e. excepted kinds, the customs authorities may ask for a declaration giving the full scientific name of the species concerned, and stating that its importation is not restricted under this Act. Importation may be restricted to specified ports, airports and border crossings, and licences may be issued on the condition that the animals are kept at specified premises.

An amendment to this Act gives power of entry to authorised persons in order to ascertain whether plants or animals are being kept illegally. A revised list of protected animals is given with the Wildlife and Countryside Act 1981.

ZOO LICENCING ACT 1981

Under this Act it is illegal to operate a zoo without first obtaining a licence from the local authority, who will first consider reports made by inspectors appointed for this purpose.

WILDLIFE AND COUNTRYSIDE ACT 1981

Among other things, this recent Act (which repeals the Conservation of Wild Creatures and Wild Plants Act 1975) gives total protection, against collection or disturbance, to the Smooth Snake, and prevents the sale, or the advertising for sale, of any other British species, except under licence.

Licences may be granted in certain circumstances, e.g. educational or scientific circumstances, photography, preserving public health and safety, etc.

It is also an offence to release or allow to escape into the wild any species which is not native.

The United States

In the United States the legal position is extremely complicated. The most important laws are the Federal laws, which apply throughout the country and which are enforced by the United States Fish and Wildlife Service. These laws are designed mainly to protect endangered North American species but some are also concerned with the importation of foreign species. (The United States is party to the Washington Convention – see above.)

In addition, there are many state and city laws and regulations and these vary greatly. Some states have hardly any restrictions on the keeping of reptiles and amphibians but in others it is banned completely. City ordinances are concerned with such matters as the keeping of dangerous species, species which are likely to become pests if released and the welfare of captive animals. If such regulations are suspected, the relevant local authority will have to be consulted.

In addition to the references given at the end of this section, information may be sought through the various regional herpetological societies and through the Society for the Study of Amphibians and Reptiles (*see* bibliography), who publish details of recent legislation through their quarterly bulletin *Herpetological Review*.

Other Countries

Many countries, e.g. Australia, have a complete ban on the importation of exotic animals, and others prohibit the capture of native species except under licence. In almost every country there are areas set aside as national parks and regulations here will almost certainly restrict the collection of reptiles and amphibians.

If the reader is in any doubt as to the legality of collecting, importing, exporting or keeping reptiles and amphibians in his or her part of the world, the only recourse is to make enquiries through the government department or local authority concerned, or by joining a local herpetological society.

Information Sources

BRITAIN

The various Acts of Parliament are usually obtainable through local lending libraries or university libraries. Alternatively, they can be ordered through bookshops acting as agents for Her Majesty's Stationery Office (most large cities have one) or directly from HMSO.

Two other useful publications obtainable from HMSO are: *Convention on International Trade in Endangered Species of Fauna and Flora* (reference number Cmnd. 5459), and *Convention on the Conservation of European Wildlife and Natural Habitats* (reference number Cmnd. 7809).

A leaflet entitled *Notice to Importers and Exporters* gives information on the Endangered Species (Import and Export) Act 1976, and is obtainable from: Wildlife Conservation Licencing Section, Department of the Environment, Tollgate House, Houlton Street, Bristol BS2 9DJ, to whom applications for licences should also be made.

UNITED STATES OF AMERICA

'Federal Registers' give details of the various federal laws and are obtainable from: Federal Wildlife Permit Office, U.S. Fish and Wildlife Service, Washington DC 20240. Further information is contained in a book entitled *A Compilation of Federal Laws Relating to Conservation and Development of our Nation's Fish and Wildlife Resources, Environmental Quality, and Oceanography*, obtainable from: The Superintendant of Documents, U.S. Government Printing Office, Washington DC 20402.

A compilation of the various state laws is contained in a publication entitled *State Laws as they pertain to Scientific Collecting Permits*, published in *Museology*, Sept. 3, 1976, No. 2. This is available from: The Museum Shop, The Museum, Texas Tech University, Lubbock, Texas 79409.

Bibliography

Listed below are a number of books and papers which have made a significant contribution to our knowledge of snake-breeding. They mostly concern techniques and general principles, since references relating to single species, or to small groups of species, are given after the sections on those species in Chapters 7–12 inclusive.

In addition to those listed, three reports, all published annually, contain a wealth of information which is invaluable to the snake-keeper, and should be regarded as essential reading.

INTERNATIONAL ZOO YEARBOOK, published by the Zoological Society of London, often contains papers on the care and breeding of snakes (some of which are listed in this book). In particular, volumes 9 and 19 (1969 and 1979) each devoted a whole section to reptiles and amphibians.

INVENTORY OF REPTILES AND AMPHIBIANS IN CAPTIVITY, compiled and published by Frank L. Slavens. This work provides far more information than its title would suggest, giving details of breeding successes by its numerous contributors, and comprehensive bibliographies. Available only through its publisher, Frank L. Slavens, P.O. Box 30744, Seattle, Washington, USA.

REPORTS OF THE INTERNATIONAL HERPETOLOGICAL SYMPOSIUM ON CAPTIVE PROPAGATION AND HUSBANDRY. These reports are the transcripts of papers given at these symposiums, the largest and most important of their kind, held annually at various venues in the United States. Several of the papers have become classic references, and these are listed separately below or in the text of this book. The report is available each year through the symposium series director, Richard A. Hahn, 13019, Catoctin Furnace Road, Thurmont, Maryland 21788, USA.

In addition, several North American and European regional societies hold occasional symposia on captive breeding, and the reports of these contain much useful information. Membership of an active society is the only sure way of finding out about them.

Coborn, J. (1977). 'Observations on the genus *Bitis*'. *Proc. Cotswold Herpetological Symposium*, 1977.

Gillingham, J. C. (1983). 'Venomous snake immobilization: a new technique'. *Herp. Review* 14(2):40.

Kauffield, C. (1969). *Snakes: The Keeper and the Kept*. Doubleday and Co., New York.

Lazlo, J. (1976). 'Practical methods of inducing mating in snakes using extended daylengths and darkness'. *Proc. 1st Ann. Symp. on Captive Propagation and Husbandry*.

Lazlo, J. (1976). 'Notes on photobiology, hibernation and reproduction in snakes'. *Proc. 1st Ann. Symp. on Captive Propagation and Husbandry*.

Lazlo, J. (1977). 'Probing as a practical method of sex recognition of reptiles, primarily snakes'. *Proc. 2nd Ann. Symp. on Captive Propagation and Husbandry*.

Lazlo, J. (1979). 'Notes on thermal requirements of reptiles and amphibians in captivity'. *Proc. 3rd Ann. Symp. on Captive Propagation and Husbandry*: 24–26.

Millichamp, N. (1980). 'Medical aspects of disease in reptile collections'. In: Townson et al, *The Care and Breeding of Captive Reptiles*, British Herpetological Society, London.

Murphy, J. B. (1971). 'A method for immobilizing venomous snakes at the Dallas Zoo'. *Int. Zoo Yb.* 11:233.

Murphy, J. B. (1980). *A Brief Outline of Suggested Treatments for Diseases of Captive Reptiles*. Society for the Study of Amphibians and Reptiles, Herpetological Circular No. 4.

Murphy, J. B. (1981). 'Maintenance of pit vipers in captivity'. *Proc. 5th Ann. Symp. on Captive Propagation and Husbandry*.

Murphy, J. B. and Collins, J. T. (Eds) (1980). *Reproductive Biology and Diseases of Captive Reptiles*. A collection of papers published by the Society for the Study of Reptiles and Amphibians.

Radcliffe, C. W. (1975). 'A method for force-feeding snakes'. *Herp. Review* 6(1):18.

Riches, R. J. (1976). *Breeding Snakes in Captivity*. Palmetto Publishing Co., Florida.

Townson, S. and Lawrence, K. (eds) (1975). *Reptiles: Breeding Behaviour and Veterinary Aspects.* A collection of papers published by the British Herpetological Society, London.

Townson, S., Millichamp, N. J., Lucas, D. G. D. and Millwood, A. J. (Eds) (1980). *The Care and Breeding of Captive Reptiles.* A collection of papers published by the British Herpetological Society, London.

Tryon, B. W. (1985). 'Snake hibernation and breeding: in and out of the zoo'. In: *Reptiles: Breeding, Behaviour and Veterinary Aspects.* British Herpetological Society, London. (Also published in *Bull. Brit. Herp. Soc.* (10):22–29 (1984).)

Wagner, E. (1976). 'Some parameters for breeding reptiles in captivity'. *Proc. 1st Ann. Symp. on Captive Propagation and Husbandry.*

Index

180